Projects in
HISTORY

Projects in
HISTORY
for the secondary school

Sheila Ferguson
Head of the History Department
Peckham Girls' School

B. T. BATSFORD LTD London

First published 1967
Second impression 1970
© Sheila Ferguson 1967

Made and printed in Great Britain
by Fletcher & Son Ltd, Norwich
for the publishers B. T. BATSFORD LTD
4 Fitzhardinge Street, London W.1

7134 2154 1

Contents

CONTENTS

PART I

History projects
and their organization

History is not Bunk

It is perhaps a paradox to begin a book about the teaching of history on a note of justification. History makes many a best-seller, historians are popular T.V. figures, and the squabbles of history dons supply ample material for the newspapers. But the theory that 'history is bunk' is far from dead and even in the schools its influence can be felt.

Few teachers, of course, would agree categorically with Henry Ford. Yet the pressure of new subjects and wider activities on the school syllabus may make history a second-class subject in the struggle for time. In the grammar schools or academic streams of other schools early specialization may decide whether history is 'in' or 'out', but even in schools less inhibited by examinations, history teaching can take on an apologetic air—it can be rendered more practical by being dressed up as 'civics', 'current affairs' or 'social studies'.

But *should* history teachers adopt this defensive posture? No doubt history as a school subject is dated, if by history we mean the patriotic mythology which filled the popular textbooks 50 years ago. This is the picture of history teaching which some adults still have in mind when they imply that other subjects should take pride of place. The other traditional view of the value of history as teaching moral lessons still remains important, even if the growth of economic and social history has undermined the concept of history as the biographies of great men. History is obviously more than that, but equally it is more than the story of tools, and we should beware of throwing out the baby with the bath water. History teaching *should* deal with moral lessons but it cannot ignore the development of the steam engine.

'We study history', said Collingwood, 'in order to see more clearly into the situation in which we are called upon to act.' An historical background is essential for the understanding of both practical and theoretical subjects. Just as it is now commonplace to claim that a liberal education without some knowledge of science is an anachronism, so should no school syllabus permit the early specialization which involves abandoning any attempt to provide pupils with some historical perspective. History is the story of humanity and the progress of society; it is the record of human behaviour and enables us to have some understanding of the present and perhaps to learn some lessons from the past. The adolescent pupil will soon be a citizen with duties and responsibilities. He should have been helped to see some connection between the world that confronts him today and the story of the struggles and aspirations of mankind. 'We are products of the past', wrote Croce, 'and we live immersed in the past that encompasses us. . . . How can we place ourselves above the past if we are in it and it is in us?'

More obviously, perhaps, history is full of drama and adventure. Man is naturally interested in what has happened before his time, and this spontaneous curiosity, so evident in the primary school, should not be allowed to wither in the secondary school through the remote and tedious presentation of material. Above all the pupil should feel that history has something to say to him, something that will interest and excite him.

Yet most teachers will admit that much history teaching has bored rather than stimulated and has failed to convey a feeling of total continuity with the past, whether in our social and political attitudes or in the way we earn our livings. No doubt a contributory factor has been that much traditional teaching has been pedestrian, uninspiring and irrelevant, especially to the less academically able children. It is here that the project method has much to offer.

The Need for a New Approach

Project work is not, of course, a new concept. It springs in part from the revolt against the 'chalk and talk' pattern of history teaching. The Dalton Plan was an extreme form of this technique, involving the abolition of the ordinary timetable in schools and cutting across subject specialization. In the primary schools, with their non-specialist class teachers, projects on such topics as transport, shelter, food or foreign countries, blending together work in English, history, geography, science and mathematics, are common practice. The secondary school should perhaps avoid repetition of such well-worn themes and plans of work, but it can use the project method successfully in other ways.

The kind of project work considered in this book involves individual children or groups of children undertaking research assignments into historical topics and producing a 'book' or modest thesis on the subjects they have chosen to investigate. The level is based roughly on the standard that can be achieved by fourth- and fifth-year secondary school children in the less academic streams, though the suggestions can easily be modified by teachers and scaled upwards or downwards for appropriate ages and abilities.

Increasing numbers of children are opting to remain at school for a fifth year, and soon this extra year will be compulsory. It is doubtful whether these children will be best served by simply carrying on with a fifth-year history syllabus which caters primarily for pupils staying on for external examinations. Teachers will be conscious of the need to review the content of the courses they offer to these children and to reconsider the suitability of traditional methods. One obvious direction is to try and get as far up-to-date as possible; there are some educationalists who go so far as to claim that only the last 50 or 60 years are at all relevant for these 15- and 16-year-olds. Another desirable development is the study of world history rather than the usual limited approach. While opinions may differ on the scope of the history syllabus, the paramount problem is to make the subject meaningful and enjoyable, and here the project method can make a useful contribution.

Children who are preparing for the General Certificate of Education examinations, and whose work is inevitably bound by the demands of an all-too-extensive syllabus, will not normally have time to devote to individual assignments of this kind (though there is a strong case for doing work on these lines with academically able children in the lower forms of the secondary school). These children, however, amount to only about 20 per cent of the fifth-year age group in the secondary schools and, when the Certificate of Secondary Education is fully established, will probably be an even lower proportion. The remaining 80 per cent or more are not tied down by such formal examination requirements and will benefit greatly, I believe, from studying history by less traditional methods. The new and more flexible C.S.E. examination has, of course, just this group of children in mind and it offers the opportunity for project work as part of the examination itself.

Projects or topics need not, of course, supplant the teaching of history chronologically or by the 'line of development' or 'patch' methods, and indeed it may seem best that projects should proceed simultaneously with normal history lessons. Thus the teacher who feels that only the last 50 years is relevant can spend half or more of his periods on recent history and in the rest of the time allow his pupils to investigate whatever topics and whatever periods they themselves find most stimulating. By continuing to study some general history with the whole class the teacher is able to encourage some sense of historical perspective and to indicate the way in which topics fit into their appropriate places. The teacher can act as a bridge or a link, putting the individual young 'specialists' in touch with each other, indicating where their interests overlap and where they can help each other with material and ideas. Above all, the teacher can stress historical continuity. Plenty of visual material in the classroom, especially time-charts and diagrams, is invaluable here.

Work along these lines has special psychological advantages of personal choice and commitment, and the opportunity to progress at an individual pace. It encourages the enquiring mind, and the child is motivated to dig more deeply into a subject he has chosen for himself. Particular problems of organization, however, confront the teacher in planning activities of this kind. Many may be daunted by the complexity of supervising separate individual projects for a large number of children and may feel the need for general guidance and advice on such matters as choice of subject, suitable reference material and the standard of work required for the C.S.E. examination. The aim of this book is to discuss the practical advantages and difficulties of the project method at classroom level. The first part of the book will consider ways of organizing the children's work and this will be followed by a number of specimen projects with reference and other source material.

Personal Choice

Perhaps the most important feature of project work in the history course is the element of personal choice. Most of us will recall that as children we found some periods and topics in history dreary and uninteresting, while others caught the imagination and were studied with enthusiasm; yet it was not the same subjects that inspired the whole class. While some, for example, regretted the passing of the Tudors, others were relieved to move on to the Stuarts; some enjoyed in detail the Hundred Years War, battle by battle, others were bored, and might well have preferred to study the houses, clothes, furniture or food of those times. In project work each child is studying a subject which he has chosen for himself and this usually means that he works with greater pleasure and enthusiasm than in a course over which he has no influence or control. Once a child has had his imagination stirred by a topic of his own choice, the interest aroused may be a lasting one. Identification with one's own subject is particularly valuable with less able children. I have experienced this on several occasions with quite backward pupils who have devoted themselves to their special subject and have lost their sense of academic inferiority by becoming an authority on it. I had one such pupil who became so committed to her work on the history of transport that she persuaded her surprised family to drive long distances on holiday to look at bridges built by Brunel!

Many children reveal unsuspected ability and interests when they are able to work at their own speed on their own subject. This question of pace is another important principle for less able children. Often such pupils have been depressed by their inability to 'keep up' with the class in academic subjects but, when they are free to write and draw at a speed they choose for themselves, the quality of their work may improve immeasurably. These 'slower' children sometimes have struggled for years to get down notes or write something up in limited periods of class time and have come to accept as inevitable that their spelling and handwriting are poor. When they are allowed to take their time there is frequently a marked improvement in their written work and a consequent raising of their morale. And the academically quicker and more able do not suffer in the least; they are not delayed while the slowest catch up, nor are they bored by unnecessary repetition.

The Rôle of the Teacher

For the teacher, however, there is no denying that projects tend to involve more exhausting work than normal class teaching. Although the work is more demanding, the results achieved are worth the effort. A class at work on individual projects is noisier and more fluid than a class where all are working on the same subject. The teacher has to be able to maintain 'order in disorder' and to allow movement, consultation, exchange of reference material and ideas, and yet at the same time to see that the talk is purposeful. An atmosphere of freedom and of cheerful concentration is the ideal. The teacher must move around among the pupils offering help and advice on material, presentation, illustration, etc. The teacher must try to remember all the children's topics and to keep eyes and ears open for useful sources of information. He must look ahead, and train the children to do so too, at the T.V. and radio programmes which may be helpful, and he must recommend suitable films, plays, exhibitions, museums, art galleries and houses to visit.

The teacher's rôle in this work is many-sided. He must stimulate and try to instil enthusiasm where response is half-hearted; he must advise, helping to give the subject a 'shape' and to define practicable limits or further avenues of exploration; he must criticize, constructively of course, and with suggestions for more research, reorganization of subject matter, and so on.

The teacher should be tutor rather than lecturer, and should be a mine of useful ideas and general knowledge on which the pupil can draw. Nevertheless, it is the pupil who should be the 'authority' on his subject and there is no need for the teacher to try to be omniscient. It is, indeed, good for the morale of the young researcher if the teacher admits frankly that he does not know a great deal about, say, the development of the internal combustion engine or the history of parks and landscape gardening, but that he would be interested to be instructed in these subjects, and that he can in any case offer one or two general suggestions.

Training in Historical Research

The project method of teaching history is, in fact, training in historical research and, if well done, is more valuable than the cramming of facts to be regurgitated at examinations. 'The pupil ceases to be a mere receptacle into which the master pours information like water into a glass', writes G. P. Gooch, 'and joyfully re-creates for himself the life, colour and movement of the past.' Ill-digested learning is soon forgotten, and in a few years history may be remembered only as something which caused one some discomfort when at school. A successful research assignment, however, may arouse the historical imagination of the pupil and he may wish to continue his studies long after the official time for the work is over.

Any system of education that encourages a child to work on his own responsibility must be advantageous. When the child enters the adult world of work he is given a job to do and a limited amount of time in which to do it and is expected to get on with it by himself. A training in the methods of research will have shown him how to find information and how to assemble the material he has acquired. The organization of his time and the carrying through of the task will have involved persistence and self-discipline.

Training in the methods of research is, however, quite a sophisticated assignment, especially if the pupils are not accustomed to this kind of activity. It is, of course, preferable if the project method is

used intermittently throughout the secondary school so that training in the techniques of research is started at an early stage. Projects
are indeed frequently done at the primary school. I was recently
impressed at the open day at my son's primary school to see that
most of the children in a class of eight-year-olds had produced a
'book' or 'centre of interest' on a topic they had chosen, with highly
individual illustrations and comments. (My son's subject was medieval warfare and, while giving scope for a small boy's fascination with
violence, it had information about the technicalities of siege weapons,
castles, machicolation and so on, mostly in the form of drawings.)

In the secondary school a useful idea would be to spend part of
one term each year in the lower part of the school on topic work,
restricted perhaps to the period currently being studied. For example, first- or second-year pupils who have been studying the
Middle Ages could be asked to choose a topic from a number suggested, and over the next few weeks in class and homework to produce an individual project folder. The choice might be for one
or more of the following subjects: costume, homes, church architecture, castles and siege warfare, arms and armour, pilgrims and pil-
grimages, monks, monasteries and friars, sports and pastimes, food,
education, farming, the merchant guilds, music and musical instruments, the development of coinage and ships. For this work a
small classroom library and a collection of postcards and illustrations from books and magazines would be needed.

As an alternative to individual projects, the work could be organized on a group basis, with three or four children combining to
produce a joint effort on their chosen topic. In this way diverse
talents for drawing, digging out information and writing up the
results can produce a happy combination. The group work can be
collated and mounted on wall charts or screens for classroom display. Or the groups might each prepare a lesson for the rest of the
class, appropriately illustrated with models, drawings, charts, diagrams or dramatic illustration, and allowing time for the class to ask
questions. Reporting back on each of the topics to the class could be
also done by individual researchers either orally or by exchanging
folders and reading each other's work.

The use of the project method in the lower forms of the secondary school seems to me valuable also as a bridge between the informal and permissive methods of learning now usual in the primary school and the more formal academic approach of the secondary school. The change of schools can be an alarming experience and consultation between the teachers in both types of school about educational aims and methods tends to be inadequate. In many primary schools there is much freedom to move about the classroom or from room to room in search of information. There is frequently opportunity for personal choice in work which proceeds at each child's individual pace. Subjects are not clearly defined and, of course, the same teacher is with the class for most of the time. From this relaxed atmosphere the child may suddenly have to accept different specialist teachers in several subjects, many of them new to him, and may have to go to a different room for each lesson. He will have to sit still at a desk and do what everyone else in his class is doing; and he will have to do it at the pace the teacher sets for everyone. It is not surprising that many children are rather overwhelmed by this complete change and find it difficult to adapt themselves to the new standards.

Choice of Subject

The first hurdle when launching a class into project work is to help each child to decide on his subject (a problem not unknown among aspiring PH.D.s). Many children find it difficult to come to a decision, while others rush in far too impulsively. At this stage the teacher must be as stimulating and keen as possible so that some of his enthusiasm for different topics can spark off a reaction in those who are actually going to do the work. It is far better, of course, to draw out suggestions from the class than to present them with a list. However, the teacher should start by mentioning some subjects that make good project material and then get the class to offer further suggestions. It is very useful at this point to take the children to browse in the school or public library in search of topics of interest. Many children at first respond apathetically to the choosing of a subject, and the teacher must then try to discover any personal interests, hobbies or convictions which might find expression. Other children too quickly choose a well-known theme which they feel will be a soft option. Some teachers feel that the organization of project work is more manageable if the number of different subjects is limited and if several children in a class work on the same one. This point of view is, I think, mistaken, as interest and enthusiasm is much greater if there is variety, and since all the work done is individual there are no satisfactory short-cuts through limitation of choice. It is, moreover, difficult to find enough books and other material to go round if a number choose to work on the same thing.

In trying to draw ideas for topics from the class, the teacher can bear in mind a number of useful stimuli. Perhaps the most obvious is to discover what other school subject the child likes or does best and then to suggest a topic in which this skill will be useful. For example, pupils good at art are able to do excellent illustrations in histories of costume, architecture or furniture; a girl who enjoys domestic science might choose to study food through the ages, or kitchens and domestic appliances; a keen geographer might apply his mapping skill to illustrations of the great voyages of discovery and exploration; a pupil good at science could study the lives of some of the great scientists; and a pupil whose only enthusiasm is sport could do a history of games and sports or of one particular sport.

Family interests or connections can also be exploited and it is wise to give the children time to talk to their parents before selecting their subject. A child from a mining family might well like to do the story of coal-mining in Britain; the granddaughter of a suffragette might choose the emancipation of women; the son of an active trade unionist might like to study working-class movements and trade unions; a policeman's child might enjoy working on the history of the police, and so on. Co-operation from the family and interest in the child's project is a help, and parents are often able to provide unusual material, illustrations, etc., on the subject, which then becomes very personal to the child. I recently had a child whose excellent project on Ancient Egypt was triggered off by the vivid reminiscences of her father who had visited some of the Egyptian temples when on army service and had gathered together a first-rate collection of postcards. Another pupil, from a religious family, chose to study the history of missionaries and missionary societies, and her whole family became deeply involved in her investigations.

Hobbies and outside interests are another source for topics. An interest in theatre, cinema, ballet, music, cars, sport, youth clubs, politics, religious organizations and so on could provide rewarding subjects. A child's future career may also suggest something. A girl intending to nurse will take a practical interest in the struggles of Florence Nightingale and her colleagues; a boy who is thinking of going into the Army might write a history of the regiment or corps he hopes to join, or follow in detail some famous military campaign; an intending telephonist might choose the history of communications or more simply the life of Alexander Graham Bell; a pupil thinking of working in a bank or insurance company might consider it useful to go into the history of these activities.

Some children look back nostalgically to a period of history which they particularly enjoyed and which they can now take up again in greater depth. Particularly nowadays, when there is a tendency to rush through ancient and even medieval history in order to reach modern times before the time comes to leave school, there are many children who would be glad to do more work on such topics as Ancient Greece or Rome, the Vikings, the medieval village, or social life in Tudor times.

Then there are always those children who claim that they are not very interested in any subject that goes at all far into the past, but who may well be attracted by a topic that is reasonably up-to-date. These children could do research on the history of space travel, the United Nations Organizations, the history of the u.s.s.r. since the Revolution, the recent history of Africa or modern China, and so on. An outstanding recent event might stir the imagination of a pupil to look into the general aspects of an immediate instance: for example, the assassination of President Kennedy might be followed up by a general study of assassination as a political phenomenon; the South

African treason trials or disturbances in the Deep South of America might suggest a study of racialism; or the death of Winston Churchill might inspire a project on the Duke of Marlborough and the Churchill family or great Prime Ministers. One pupil of mine did a most interesting project on the history of the persecution of the Jews after seeing the film *Exodus*.

Even when all these avenues have been conscientiously explored the teacher may well find himself with a number of 'don't knows' on his hands. He must then persevere with further suggestions and use great ingenuity and patience to get some response from these 'difficult' children. I found, for instance, a very tough young Cockney with a real nostalgia for the country. Her grandmother had moved to London from Norfolk years ago but had such a fund of stories of country life that the child was happy to work on a history of farming, especially since Norfolk played such an important part in the agrarian revolution. A girl obsessed with horses threw herself into the history of man's use of the horse with great enthusiasm. First- and second-generation immigrants from the West Indies or from Cyprus or Pakistan might well enjoy a study of the history of their country of origin.

It is always a depressing experience if many children choose to do the same well-worn topics and very few come up with original ideas. It is monotonous if the bulk of the class chooses great lives, costume and transport, and one is bound to feel that many of the children have made their choice out of lack of imagination or indifference and because these topics are straightforward and well-documented.

Even if five girls in the class are determined to 'do' Florence Nightingale, it may be possible to persuade some of them to widen their subject and to introduce more variety. For example, one might be encouraged to link the study with a more detailed account of the Crimean War, and another might go into conditions in the army in the nineteenth century and earlier; or Florence Nightingale could be contrasted with other pioneering women such as Elizabeth Fry, Elizabeth Garrett Anderson, Mary Kingsley, etc., or she could be considered in the perspective of a history of advances in medical and hospital services.

The Technique of Research

While the choice of subjects is still being explored and many children are undecided, the teacher must begin to discuss with the pupils the methods of historical 'research'. The children are often inclined to think that finding themselves a book on their subject and then diligently copying out chunks of it is all that is required. The teacher must explain, and possibly illustrate with examples, how to collect and collate material from several sources and how to write a continuous narrative embodying the most useful and interesting information acquired. This skill in assembling information from a variety of sources to form a coherent story is a difficult one to master. Children should be trained to do this, in any case, as part of their general history course, when they can be asked to answer questions or write essays using two or more text and reference books. The teacher should explain the need to take notes from several books and emphasize that the pupil should not rush into writing a final version at too early a stage.

One of the surprises to many children is that there can be more than one version of a piece of history and that variations in emphasis and even in facts can present the subject in quite a different light. They must learn to make comparisons between different accounts and to be able to explain that while some historians claim this, other commentators disagree and one must accordingly consider their alternative interpretations. It is real success if the young researcher reaches the point of saying 'Some people believe . . . so and so; others argue . . . this and that; but on balance I think . . . this.'

Another aspect of the technique of research that has to be emphasized is the need for putting down the story in the pupil's own words. The teacher must always emphasize that the pupil should never accept words or complicated phrases which will only sound stilted and unnatural. The book may say ponderously that the 'working-classes lived in the vicinity of the reeking temples of industry'; the pupil should say that 'the workers lived near the smoky factories'. He can, of course, if he finds such phrases or passages especially colourful or expressive, use the actual words in quotation marks and keep a record of his source.

Many teachers are unnecessarily alarmed about plagiarism. (Tom Lehrer's satirical song 'Lobachevsky' makes the point that academic success at university level may well be gained by assimilating and collating the discoveries of other people.) They claim that children working on projects do no original work and are merely copying from other people's books—a worthless exercise. This point of view is unrealistic. Much reputable non-fiction is in fact a 'scissors-and-paste' operation, and the amount of new thinking and original research is small, even in academic circles. The children must, however, be taught never to copy unthinkingly and not to use words which sound pompous and artificial; above all, they should never use a word or expression whose meaning is not absolutely clear to them. The teacher can easily demonstrate this to a pupil by reading aloud a few sentences which sound stilted and by asking what is meant by 'social mobility' or 'longevity', for example. Dictionaries and a thesaurus should be kept to hand to find alternative words and expressions when needed. The children should be urged to reach a personal conclusion wherever possible and to sum up their views on the subject in their own words.

After emphasizing the point about 'own words' recently I was surprised and pleased, when a pupil showed me her folder, to find that she had decided to write the history of power (in the sense of energy) as different contemporaries might have recorded their impressions. She wrote about James Watt and steam power as seen through the eyes of Matthew Boulton and Edmund Cartwright, about Michael Faraday and Alexander Graham Bell as seen by their friends, and so right up to the splitting of the atom and nuclear power. The work was imaginative in its writing but factual in information, and is one of the most interesting projects I have seen.

The importance of keeping careful records of their sources of information must be continually stressed to the pupils. They need to keep a running list of books consulted as they make their notes: it will be no use later to think that it was a 'fat green book' that was used to give some information which the pupil now wants to follow up or quote in his final account. Cuttings from magazines or news-papers should be marked clearly with the name of the periodical and its date, and a file of notes, snippets, possible illustrations, etc., should be part of the researcher's tools. In this folder he can keep together anything which may ultimately be of use to the project, including notes on museums and other places of interest visited, notes on historical novels read, plays and television programmes seen, and so on.

Giving the Topic a Shape

After the project has been in progress for a few weeks and the children have had time to browse on their subjects and to get some ideas on how to tackle the work, the teachers should get each pupil to produce a rough plan of the headings or chapters under which the study will be written. The teacher should emphasize at the outset the need to read as widely as possible before putting pen to paper in any final way. Most children want to rush in and write an introduction first of all and they are surprised when it is suggested that it is probably best to write the introduction last, when all the information has been collected and written up. Only when the researcher has got a complete picture of his material is he able to indicate in an introduction what his work is going to cover. The introduction and the conclusion can both be written in the final stages.

The importance of making notes from several sources has been stressed. Only when a substantial body of information has been collected should the pupil proceed to the next stage which is to plan the 'shape' of the study. The pupil should now have some idea about the scope and limits of his proposed project—for instance, how far back and how far up-to-date he wants to go—and the teacher should be able to advise about the practicability of the scheme. The teacher may find the plan too ambitious or too modest, unmanageably long or likely to be too soon exhausted, and can suggest ways of limiting an over-large subject and ways of extending one that seems rather narrow.

This stage of drawing up skeleton plans of section or chapter headings is a vital one in project work. Schemes can always, of course, be altered and can be added to or reduced, but a good, clear plan of work at an early stage is a valuable discipline. It makes the organization of work more manageable than when material is collected and collated in a haphazard way. Such skeleton plans of work are the essential bones of the specimen projects set out later in the book.

Once the shape of the project has been decided the child can use the headings for keeping his research material in order. As he finds that he has enough information for any particular section he can write it up in more or less final form, even if it is out of order in the work. In this way a child need not be held up by a missing book or by some stone unturned or gap unfilled. A student of the history of roads, for instance, could write up the recent developments in motorways and mount his maps and illustrations for this section even though he was still dissatisfied with the material he had collected on the Turnpike Trusts and the great era of stage coaches.

It is partly because I find it better if the children do not have to begin at the beginning and write straight through to the end in their topics, that I urge children to do their projects on loose-leaf paper rather than in books. Additional information, even for a section that was believed to be complete, can then be slipped in later and odd pages can be written and new illustrations included. For this reason I also discourage the writing up of projects in formal chapters but rather suggest sections to which additional material can be added at any time.

Although each child should be free to present his work in whatever form appeals to him, the teacher should also, where necessary, advise on lay-out and presentation. This is an aspect of project work, however, that usually presents few problems as most children take a pride in the appearance of their work and are happy to cover their folders neatly and to do attractive lettering and illustrations. The less academic child with some artistic ability can often make up for a somewhat thin folder on the written side by producing one lavishly illustrated and presented with loving care. The child who does not enjoy drawing, however, can be reassured that his work, with less illustration but more 'meat', is just as valuable.

Help in Gathering Material

Once some preliminary work has been done on choice of subjects and on advice about the methods of historical research, the members of the class should be given time and as much help as possible to get on with their individual assignments. Some class time is essential for project work though in fact most children who have chosen a satisfactory topic will be very willing to do extra work at home. For example, two girls chose as their topic the history of the Tower of London and developed a passion for the subject. Although they lived some distance away in south London, they used to walk to and from the Tower Saturday after Saturday and spend a good deal of the day there. They explored in every detail the actual stones and fabric of the building whose history they were writing. They became well-known to several of the Yeoman Warders and included their autographs in the folders. I even got them to read Josephine Tey's *Daughter of Time* for an alternative picture of Richard III and the murder of the Princes in the Tower, but they were unimpressed by the case and preferred the more traditional view of Richard's villainy. They worked together on the same subject for their project folders but the writing up of each was an individual effort. Each of their folders was a work of love and I am sure that they will be treasured in the years to come and probably enjoyed by their children.

The teacher must carry in his head, as far as possible, all the subjects being done and keep eyes and ears open for any useful material for work in progress. Most children have a squirrel instinct and love collecting and amassing postcards, pictures and cuttings, and they greatly appreciate any contributions to their hoards. The newspaper colour supplements, the *Listener* and other weekend reviews, magazines such as *Country Life*, and old B.B.C. pamphlets on radio and television programmes for schools are all valuable sources of illustrations.

Visits to museums, public buildings and 'stately homes' in the neighbourhood should be organized where possible, and here again the children usually gather a good haul of postcards or other illustrations. Teaching in London, I find the possible number of visits enormous and, as whole classes can only be taken out occasionally, I urge the older children to make these visits at the weekends with a friend or to get their family to take them. Most of the museums are extremely helpful both to whole classes and to individual children doing research. On one occasion the curator of the Geffrye Museum, for example, provided male and female period costumes which volunteer models from my class wore while the rest sketched them against the background of the appropriately furnished room. The London Museum, on being approached by a girl writing about the suffragettes, produced from their archives some original photographs not then on display and had them reproduced for her.

I have included details of many useful museums, historic buildings and other places of interest throughout. Some of the most useful sources for a particular project may be at an impossible distance for the child concerned, but if a pupil knows about the place it is sometimes possible to make the visit while on holiday or during a school journey, or the child may care to write and ask for an illustrated catalogue or postcards.

One early essential in this work is to get each child to join the public library. Many will, of course, already belong, but some will not and it must be emphasized that, however good the school library may be and however many books the history teacher has collected, there can never be enough material for most of the subjects. It is sometimes difficult to persuade some of the older children that the best source of reading matter for their projects is the Children's Library. Often children who were members of the Library in the primary school regard the Children's Library as a place for little children who want story books, and yet they are not really up to using the Adult Library and so have let their membership lapse. This is a problem which I understand is exercising the minds of some librarians. The Lambeth Children's Librarian, who has done some interesting work in recommending suitable reading for adolescents, told me of some possible solutions librarians have in mind. The teacher should emphasize that the Children's Library usually has excellent material for history project work—better in fact than the Adult section—and the librarians are most co-operative in finding suitable books for those who ask for help. Even if the branch has nothing on the subject in question, an appropriate book can usually be recommended and can be obtained from another library on payment of the cost of a stamp for the notification card. I have found children most impressed by this service.

The existence of a fully equipped History Room with a library of its own and facilities for visual aids is invaluable, though in many schools such provision is still a far-distant ideal. If, however, the teacher concerned in project work teaches the class or classes in question from the same base, it is usually possible to make good use of the wall-space and to have a cupboard with reference books and other equipment. I have found it useful to have a Time Line as a frieze along one wall, and then with pieces of coloured tape to connect the line to a lively illustration or piece of writing borrowed from a pupil's topic folder. One must be careful not to spoil the work on display; the use of photographic corners and covering the page with plastic film or cellophane will prevent it getting dirty. Thus the whole class can see aspects of various topics in their time perspective and have a chance to look at other subjects than their own. And the proud author or illustrator has a wider public for his work.

A classroom library for project work done in class time and to supply books on loan for private study is invaluable, and it is usually possible to build up a good collection fairly quickly. There are a number of very useful series such as the Methuen's Outline Series, the Longmans' 'Then and There' Series, the Hamish Hamilton 'Look at . . . ' Series, the E.S.A. Information books, the U.L.P. 'Discovering the . . . ' Series, and the Batsford books on costume and architecture. I also add odd copies of history textbooks, a number of simple biographies and a selection of paperback historical novels for background reading.

The use of contemporary documents and other direct sources is most valuable and I have found that the children are always impressed by seeing what the 'real thing' looked like and by reading the actual comments of the people who experienced the events at the time. The excellent Jackdaw Series from Jonathan Cape provides impressive documentary evidence and information on many topics. For example, in Jackdaw No. 8, facsimile pages from William Bradford's diary list the names of those who sailed in the *Mayflower*, when they were married, had children and died, and is much more alive and memorable than just reading the bald fact that 120 pilgrims sailed. The actual names of husbands, wives and children who died in the 'general sickness' of the first winter makes more impact than simply reading that half the pilgrims died then. The Longmans 'Then and There' Series also approaches many of its subjects from the specific example and is usually very helpful on source material. Bland, Brown and Tawney's *Select Economic Documents* and other such collections provide a mine of quotable documentary evidence.

Sometimes the children produce an original document or photograph from family sources to illustrate their subject. A pupil working on the history of Lambeth recently produced the following letter from the Board of Guardians to her grandfather:

PARISH OF LAMBETH, BOARD OF GUARDIANS

Guardians' Office,
Brook Street,
Kennington, S.E.
17th August, 1927.

Dear Sir,

The Guardians have had under consideration the question of taking legal proceedings to recover the amount of out-relief advanced by way of loan during the General Strike in May, 1926.

According to my ledger there is the sum of 1/- still due from you, which I shall be glad to receive at an early date so as to avoid the possibility of proceedings being taken against you in respect thereof.

Yours faithfully,
E. A. Green
(Collector)

She included the letter in her project folder and I took a photostat to use when teaching about the Welfare State!

In addition to the books one is able to collect for a classroom library, I have found that my local library is willing to supplement our reference material by allowing us to borrow on long loan a number of books that I select. I also have a collection of magazines such as *Knowledge*, *Finding Out*, *Look and Learn*, guides to museums and historic buildings and a collection of postcards from museums and art galleries. A good supply of stationery—folders, paper, coloured pencils, glue and adhesive tape—is also essential.

Many children gain great satisfaction if they can get help on their project from some outside organization. They enjoy writing to public bodies, government departments, associations or firms, saying that they are doing some research on a subject and asking if the organization has any information or illustrations that might help. Most of the children I have taught who have tried this have met with considerable co-operation. Among those who have sent useful material to my young researchers have been the Ministry of Health (on public health and nursing), the Department of Education and Science, the Trades Union Congress and two individual trade unions, the National Coal Board, the B.B.C., our local Borough Council, the British Transport Commission and one or two firms, such as Marconi. One of my pupils wrote to the Elizabeth Garrett Anderson Hospital for information about its founder and was invited to visit the hospital; there she was seen personally by the matron and shown round. Many organizations now have public relations departments with much hand-out material available; they appreciate the children's interest and think it is worth taking a little trouble to be of help. Some big firms have had their histories written for them by professional historians and are willing to send background information to children who write to them.

Some children prefer to research into a topic which seems rather obscure and not much covered in the books immediately available. These children often have a strong 'detective' instinct and prefer the challenge of the hunt rather than following the more obvious and well-worn paths. Their work may have to be the pursuit of clues from book to book and the gathering of snippets. Although the folders of these children will tend to be less full than those of children who have chosen more straightforward subjects, their enterprise and the value of their training in research will make up for the small quantity. Examples I have encountered of this type of subject include the history of public libraries, of advertisement posters and of heating and lighting.

Historical Fiction

As well as using direct reference material, it is a good idea to encourage children to read historical novels set in the periods they are studying. Contemporary novels, such as those by Defoe, Dickens, Mrs Gaskell, Charles Kingsley and the Brontës, are valuable source material but children often find them hard going. There are, however, many good modern writers of historical fiction for children whose books provide a valuable atmosphere. A list of suggested suitable historical fiction is given on page 118. Even if a historical novel is not relevant enough to quote from, I suggest that the book should be included in the bibliography as a help in getting the feel of the period. The pupil might even like to include brief reviews of the background fiction he has read and criticize or praise the novels he feels to be either inaccurate or particularly true to life. For example, a child writing about Oliver Cromwell and the Parliamentary cause might comment on the undue weight of sympathy for the Royalists. Reviews of plays, films or television programmes relevant to particular studies might also be included in the project folder.

Final Stages of the Work

Sometimes a subject which has been worked on for some time goes sour on a child, his work tails off or he wants to change his topic, and a salvage operation of some kind is needed. The teacher must now either suggest a quick change of subject or try to help liven up the original choice with some new ideas. It is better, of course, if this sort of problem is avoided altogether by careful selection of subjects at the outset, but in spite of every care mistakes are bound to be made and it is against the purpose of the activity to drive a very unwilling horse. Girls, for example, often feel that enthusiasm for current fashions means that they will enjoy doing a study of historical fashions, but they sometimes get bogged down in recording the detailed descriptions of clothes that they may have drawn with pleasure. The intricate, technical accounts of costumes can be daunting to those who are not experts in the field. In this situation I find it is helpful to suggest a widening of scope by introducing a new but relevant interest. For instance, a girl who has worked herself to a standstill on eighteenth-century costume could decide not to press on with costume in the nineteenth and twentieth centuries but to study instead eighteenth-century backgrounds for her clothes. She could consider eighteenth-century furniture, houses and/or the theatre, could link these up and perhaps bring out some relationship between them and the work already done on costume. Another possibility would be to study contemporary writing for descriptions and opinions of clothes, furniture, houses, food and so on. Chaucer, the Paston letters, Pepys, Fanny Burney, Jane Austen and Dickens are obvious sources for this sort of material. More suggestions for extending a chosen topic are given throughout this book.

It is very difficult to offer any useful advice about the size of history projects. Some subjects are not well covered in suitable books while in others there is a wealth of useful material. Some children can write briefly but clearly while others are more wordy. Some concentrate most on illustrations, others on writing. And it is difficult to assess blindfold the weight that should be given to quality rather than quantity. However, for my pupils who present projects for their C.S.E. examination, I usually say that I regard 25 written sheets (or 50 pages), apart from illustrations, as a minimum requirement. Most of the pupils in fact produce considerably more written work than this.

All authors need the stimulus of a date-line for the completion of their work, and children too must have a target for 'going to press';

otherwise there is a danger that the job will never get finished. If the folders are to be assessed and given a mark as part of the C.S.E. examination the incentive to finish is obvious but, even when there is no pressure of external examination, project folders can be counted as part of the year's marks for an internal history course. It may be a good idea to offer a prize or two for the best projects, or perhaps to put a year's topic work on show at a parents' evening or within the school. Authors and artists usually produce their work for others to read or see and they appreciate interest in their efforts. The teacher, too, may find it useful to have his pupils' projects looked at by outside teachers or inspectors who can assess the standard of work with more detachment.

Suggested Topics

The following is a list of possible subjects. Many more will readily spring to mind. Often a part of one of the headings suggested will be sufficient in itself for an assignment. Some of the subjects are dealt with in detail in Part II.

History of costume. Fashions. Armour.

Buildings—homes, houses, castles, church architecture.

Inside the home—furniture, the kitchen, food, gardens.

Education and schools.

Sports and pastimes. Holidays.

Entertainments—theatre, cinema, ballet, opera.

Transport and travel. Roads. Railways. Canals. Ships. Wheeled vehicles. The internal combustion engine. Flight. Undersea travel.

The life of children through the ages. The care of young children.

The emancipation of women.

Poverty. The care of old people.

Farming and country life. Domestic animals and pets.

Medicine and public health. Nursing.

Communication—wireless, telephone, television, newspapers.

Postal services.

The development of industry, or particular industries, e.g. cotton, iron and steel, chemical, pottery.

Inventions. Lives of great inventors.

Science and scientific discoveries.

The history of the study of the solar system.

Space exploration, rockets.

The art of war—in ancient times, medieval warfare, siege weapons, castles, weapons, knights and their armour. Sea warfare.

The development of explosives.

The story of the atom. The development of nuclear power.

Systems of government. The history of Parliament in England.

The development of coinage.

Local government.

World organizations.

Local history.

Trade unions and working-class movements.

Exploration. Maps and mapmakers. Great explorers, voyages of discovery.

Police. Law and order.

Fire services.

Studies of life in particular periods—life in Ancient Greece or Rome, in Roman Britain, Anglo-Saxon England. The Vikings. Life in Britain in the Middle Ages. Life under the Tudors and Stuarts. Victorian England. The early history of America. Studies of epic periods in history—the Crusades, the Armada, the English Civil War, the American Civil War, the French Revolution, the Irish Question.

The American Indians.

Music and musicians.

Painters and sculptors.

The slave trade.

Prehistory, early man, archaeological discoveries.

World War I.

World War II.

The history of the British Commonwealth or parts of it—India, Australia, etc.

Dictatorship. The rise of Hitler and Mussolini.

The Russian Revolution and after.

The new Africa.

China in the twentieth century.

Modern Israel.

Nasser and Egypt.

Racialism and its problems.

Banks. Insurance.

Great lives—reformers, explorers, inventors, writers, statesmen, women, etc.

PART II

Specimen projects

THE SKELETON PLANS which follow have been chosen to illustrate the way in which work might be organized on a number of typical subjects, to discuss the material that might be incorporated and to make suggestions about sources of information. Only about 20 of the many possible subjects have been explored in this way, but they have been selected as those likely to be popular and as examples which should be helpful to teachers called on for advice about many other similar topics. Although the plans are in note or 'skeleton' form, in another sense they are 'ideal' in that the schemes of work they suggest, if developed in any depth, are more comprehensive than those that could be expected from most children. The headings in the plans have been set out in greater detail than should be necessary in the average child's project, in order to give the teacher suitable and organized background information on the selected topics.

It goes without saying that the teacher should not spoon-feed the pupil by offering ready-made plans. Indeed, it is entirely contrary to the purpose of the activity, if the teacher rather than the child does the planning. However, from the material provided, the teacher should be able to comment on the pupil's scheme and make suggestions for improvements, even if this is a topic with which he is not familiar.

Medicine and Public Health

This is a very big subject covering man's struggle to survive, from superstition and witchcraft right up to modern scientific discoveries. The pupil must either attempt to cover the whole field very briefly or must select sections for more detailed consideration. It will first be necessary to read a general account of the history of medicine, to draw up a list of headings and then to decide on the limits of the project. Three useful books to start on are *Medicine* by J. Boswell Taylor (E.S.A.), *From Magic to Medicine* by Ritchie Calder (Rathbone Books) and *Disease and Medicine* by R. W. Johnson (Batsford), as well as the appropriate sections of the children's encyclopaedias. It is perhaps more practicable to limit a study to developments from the seventeenth century onwards, with just a brief section on earlier ideas, methods and conditions.

A comprehensive set of headings might be:

1. Magic and superstition.
2. Medicine in early civilizations: Sumeria, Babylonia, Hammurabi's Code, Egypt.
3. Greek medicine: Hippocrates and Aesculapius. Medicine moves from mystery to science. The Hippocratic Oath.
4. The Romans. Drains and water supplies, public health.
5. The Dark Ages. Return to superstition. Barber-surgeons, herbalists, apothecaries.
6. Lack of hygiene in medieval times. Epidemic diseases. The Black Death.
7. The Renaissance. Medicine flourishes again. Leonardo da Vinci.
8. Early hospitals.

Items 1–8 could be used in a brief introduction and the story continued from here in more detail.

9. The seventeenth century: great strides in medicine. Harvey and the circulation of the blood. Thomas Sydenham and epidemic diseases. The Royal Society.
10. Edward Jenner and smallpox vaccination.
11. The conquest of pain. Laughing gas and ether. Joseph Priestley, Sir Humphry Davy, William Morton, James Simpson.
12. Florence Nightingale and the reform of nursing.
13. Louis Pasteur and germs.
14. Joseph Lister and antiseptics.
15. Public health in the nineteenth century. Chadwick. Cholera epidemics. The Public Health Acts.
16. Röntgen and x-rays.
17. The Curies and radium.

18. Sir Ronald Ross and yellow fever.
19. New drugs. Sulphonamides.
20. Sir Alexander Fleming and penicillin.
21. The National Health Scheme.
22. Medicine today. Recent advances, heart transplants, etc.

Recommended Books

A Short History of Medicine, F. N. L. Poynter and K. D. Keele
  (Mills & Boon)
Medicine through the Ages, G. R. Davidson (Methuen)
The Story of Nursing, J. M. Calder (Methuen)
Men Who Found Out, A. Williams-Ellis (Bodley Head)—Lister, the
  Curies, Reed, etc.
Changing the World, A. Williams-Ellis (Bodley Head)—Fleming,
  Rutherford
Men Who Shaped the Future, E. Larsen (Phoenix House)—
  Fleming, Florey, etc.
Laughing Gas and the Safety Lamp, A. Williams-Ellis and E. Cooper
  Willis (Methuen)
Social Reformers, N. Wymer (Oxford)—for Florence Nightingale
People Who Mattered, G. Pocock (Dent)—for Florence Nightingale
Florence Nightingale, E. White (Cassell)
Florence Nightingale, L. R. Seymer (Faber)
Lady-in-Chief, C. Woodham-Smith (Methuen)
Elizabeth Garrett Anderson, J. Manton (Methuen); and by N. Wymer
  (Muller)
Medical Scientists and Doctors, N. Wymer (Oxford)—Harvey,
  Pasteur, Lister, Garrett Anderson, Pavlov, Curie, Fleming, etc.
Six Great Doctors, J. G. Crowther (Hamish Hamilton)—Harvey,
  Lister, Ross, Pasteur, Pavlov, Fleming
The Radium Woman, E. Doorly (Heinemann)
Marie Curie, R. McKnown (Black)
Joseph Lister, E. Jenkins (Nelson)
Edward Jenner, Conqueror of Smallpox, J. Boswell Taylor (Mac-
  millan)

The Microbe Man, E. Doorly (Heinemann)—Pasteur
Louis Pasteur, N. Pain (Black)
The Mosquito Man: the Story of Sir Ronald Ross, J. Rowland (Lutterworth)
The Penicillin Man: the Story of Sir Alexander Fleming, J. Rowland (Lutterworth)
The Chloroform Man: the Story of Dr James Simpson, J. Rowland (Lutterworth)
The Polio Man: the Story of Dr Salk, J. Rowland (Lutterworth)
All About Great Men of Medicine, R. F. Hume (W. H. Allen)
Humphry Davy: 'Pilot of Penzance', J. Kendall (Faber)
Great Company: the Fight Against Disease, P. Chambers (Bodley Head)
I Swear and Vow: the Story of Medicine, E. J. Trimmer (Blond Educational)
Man's War Against Germs, A. Hill and S. Ault (Heinemann)

Sources of information

The Ministry of Health, Whitehall, London s.w.1—on public health and nursing
The British Medical Association, Tavistock Square, London w.c.1
General Nursing Council for England and Wales, 23 Portland Place, London w.1

Museums

Wellcome Historical Medical Museum, Euston Road, London N.W.1 (child welfare, Jenner, Lister, Pasteur, etc.)
The Science Museum, Exhibition Road, South Kensington, London s.w.7
Royal College of Surgeons Museum, 183 Euston Road, London N.W.1
Anatomical Museum, University New Buildings, Edinburgh 8

Law and Order

This is a subject in which the pupil might be encouraged to widen the scope of his original idea of the history of the police, or of crime and punishment, or of prisons and prison reform, or of capital punishment. Recently, for instance, I had a rather difficult pupil whose only suggestion for a project was 'the history of torture'. I accepted this, which was chosen mainly to shock, and then gently encouraged her to extend the study to crime and punishment through the ages, including prison reform.

The first need in starting subjects of this general nature is to define the terms. Often a junior or children's dictionary gives more direct and understandable definitions than the more comprehensive volumes for adults. For example, the *Thorndike Junior Dictionary* defines 'Law' as 'A rule made by a country, state, etc. A system of rules formed to protect society'; and 'Order' as 'A state or condition of things in which law is obeyed and there is no trouble'.

To maintain law and order, the punishment of wrongdoers is introduced as a deterrent. This dates back from the earliest times, ever since men began to live in groups. It is important to make clear to the pupil that there is a distinction between the government making the law and the police seeing that the law is observed and the judges and courts of law trying alleged breaches of the law. More definitions are needed here, as it is most important for the child to see the distinction between passing laws, maintaining law and order, and punishing when the law is broken.

The next stage is for the child to consult an encyclopaedia or reference book and so to draw up a sketch plan for the project. The teacher can help to amplify where necessary. Below is the outline of a comprehensive scheme which could be attempted, as a whole or in part.

1. Definitions. The scope of the project.
2. Early law. The family and primitive communities did not need a police force, but as society grew more complex and more

mobile, it became necessary to make laws and to see they were kept. Connection between law and religion.

3. Early law and order in Britain. The Romans—Pax Romana. The Anglo-Saxons—shire moots, trial by ordeal.
4. Keeping the law in the Middle Ages. Manorial Courts. Constables. Hue and Cry. Judges and Justices of the Peace. Witchcraft.
5. Law and order under the Tudors and Stuarts. The poor and the parish. Harsh punishments. The Court of Star Chamber.
6. Lawlessness in the eighteenth century. Highwaymen. The Bow Street runners. Transportation.
7. Sir Robert Peel and the new police.
8. The police in the twentieth century.
9. Ideas on punishment—'an eye for an eye, a tooth for a tooth' of the Old Testament gradually being modified. Very harsh punishment of the sixteenth century, etc.—capital punishment for stealing, whipping, mutilation, torture, stocks and pillory, prison, transportation, fines, probation.
10. Penal reform. Prisons originally for people awaiting trial or execution, also for debtors until they paid their debts. Houses of Correction in the sixteenth century for rogues and vagabonds, where they worked and received training. Very bad conditions in gaols; epidemics. Descriptions in the novels of Fielding and Goldsmith. John Howard's efforts. Elizabeth Fry. Recent views and reforms. Abolition of capital punishment.
11. Treatment of young offenders. Age of responsibility. Juvenile courts, approved schools, probation, etc.

Recommended Books

Law and Order, J. Dumpleton (Black)—excellent account
Policeman, J. Chillingworth (Lutterworth)—useful introduction
The Policeman, N. Bebbington (E.S.A.)
Discovering the Law, J. Derriman (U.L.P.)
Hue and Cry, P. Pringle (Museum Press)
Penal Reform in England, ed. P. H. Winfield (Macmillan)

Law and Order, B. Ashley (Batsford)
The Courts of Justice, W. J. Jenkins (Wheaton)
Police and Prisons, P. F. Speed (Longmans)
Elizabeth Fry, E. White (Cassell)
Elizabeth Fry, K. Barne (Methuen)
999 Police, J. Boswell Taylor (Walrus Books)
Crime and Society, B. Whitaker (Blond)

Costume or Fashion

This is an obvious choice for many girls who feel that their keen interest in current fashions makes a history of clothes a good subject for them to investigate. It can, however, prove disappointing, as enthusiasm can be easily blunted when the time comes to write up the detailed technical descriptions of costume that need to go with the drawings that have been done with such pleasure. To avoid this problem the teacher should try from the outset to encourage the pupil to keep illustrations and written work in reasonable balance. The teacher should also point out that much of the detail is only necessary for specialists and that the important things to note are the main *trends* in fashion. A glossary of technical and foreign words might be a useful section in the work and avoid constant explanations. The teacher can show the child by example how to simplify an unduly complicated description and make it more in her own idiom. For example, a passage in *English Costume of the Nineteenth Century* by I. Brooke and J. Laver, describing 'evening toilettes' 1885–1890 says: '*Décolletage* was not extreme. After being eclipsed for a time by the *décolleté en cœur*, the square opening came back into favour, although for those who were afraid of being thought too thin the round opening was preferred. White gloves were, of course, *de rigueur*, and precious stones, particularly diamonds, were worn in great numbers. . . . ' This might be summarized as: 'Evening dresses were not cut very low and had square, heart-shaped or round necks. White gloves were worn and much jewellery.'

The best way to begin on this topic is to give the child several books on costume and any well-illustrated history textbooks and magazines and let her browse and choose the period that she likes best. The subject is such a big one with such a wealth of material that it is essential to decide on the limits of the study at an early stage, though it can, of course, always be extended or reduced. Some children like to attempt a 'right-through' history of clothes from cave men to the present day in which they only pick out a few descriptions of clothes from before 1066 and then a few examples of the main trends in each century. Others prefer to study one or two centuries in greater depth and they often take great pleasure in getting as far up to date as possible.

This is not a subject in which much skeleton planning is needed, as once the chronological limits of the study have been set it is usually a question of drawing and describing the fashion changes for each five, 10, 20, 50 or 100 years. It should, however, be emphasized that there are innumerable aspects that need to be mentioned whenever possible—what materials were used and where they came from, what colours were fashionable, what stockings and shoes, what hats and gloves were worn, what the hair styles were like and what accessories were carried, what under-garments were worn, etc., etc.

As well as providing a number of books on costume, such as those listed below, it is also useful to have postcard reproductions of pictures with clear detail of costume from the National Portrait Gallery, the National Gallery, and other art galleries and museums. If a child is describing seventeenth-century clothes and has listed the main characteristics and drawn a typical example from one of the specialist books, she could then examine, for instance, the portrait of Henrietta Maria by G. Honthorst or Charles I by Daniel Mytens (National Portrait Gallery) and decide how fashionable or unfashionable they were. She could give detailed descriptions of the clothes in the portraits, using some of the technical terms she has learnt, and hazard a guess about material, padding, stiffening, etc.

The teacher may like to suggest to the pupil that she gives her personal comments on the clothes she is describing—are they pretty or elegant? comfortable? washable? practicable? Are any recent fashions comparable (e.g. the 'Teddy Boys' and the Edwardian dandies, the pop groups who wore 'Tom Jones' bows and frilled shirts, or the revival of the 1920 line in women's clothes)? How are the clothes made? Were fashions different for the rich and the poor and if so how?

I have usually found that it is wisest for the pupil to limit her project in the first instance to a fairly short period, say a century; then it can later be extended backwards or forwards if necessary. If interest flags it will be easy to suggest that the topic might now include other related subjects such as housing, furniture or the theatre of the same period. An interesting comparative study might then be made of taste and design in, for example, eighteenth-century clothes, Chippendale and Hepplewhite furniture, the Adam brothers' houses, and even perhaps the music of Handel and Mozart.

Another possible line to explore is contemporary opinions and descriptions of clothes in journals, letters, novels or plays written at the time chosen for study. Chaucer, Pepys, Evelyn, Fanny Burney and Jane Austen are obvious sources, while a dictionary of quotations might provide one or two good snippets from poets such as Herrick and Suckling.

Some pupils may like to investigate such topics as methods of spinning and weaving cloth, the production of different kinds of material, dyeing, printing and the like. Help can perhaps be obtained by writing to the International Wool Secretariat, 18-20 Regent Street, London W.1, or similar organizations.

Methods of making clothes might also be worth attention—from the picture painted in Hood's *Song of the Shirt* and Kingsley's *Alton Locke* of seamstresses' life to the introduction of the sewing machine and the mass production of clothing. Elias Howe in 1841 produced the first workable sewing machine but there were many other versions and subsequent improvements.

Museums

Victoria and Albert Museum, South Kensington, London S.W.7
    (a fine collection of costumes, several well-illustrated booklets, and
    postcards)

London Museum, Kensington Palace, London w.8 (royal robes)
Gallery of English Costume, Platt Hall, Manchester
Mrs D. Langley Moore's Collection, Bath, Somerset
Kirkstall Abbey House Museum, Leeds
Bethnal Green Museum, Cambridge Heath Road, London e.2 (especially dolls)
Lewis Textile Museum, Blackburn, Lancashire (spinning and weaving)
Luton Museum, Wardown Park, Luton, Bedfordshire (straw hats)
Museum of Costume, Eridge Castle, Tunbridge Wells, Kent
Canongate Tolbooth, Edinburgh 8 (Highland dress)

Recommended Books

Discovering Costume, A. I. Barfoot (U.L.P.)—very good introduction, clear and simple
Look at Clothes, P. Binder (Hamish Hamilton)—simple but good for ideas and generalizations
Costume, J. Laver (Batsford)
English Costume, I. Brooke (Methuen)
English Children's Costume since 1775, I. Brooke (Black)
English Costume in the Early Middle Ages, I. Brooke (Black)
English Costume in the Later Middle Ages, I. Brooke (Black)
English Costume in the Age of Elizabeth, I. Brooke (Black)
English Costume in the Seventeenth Century, I. Brooke (Black)
English Costume in the Eighteenth Century, I. Brooke and J. Laver (Black)
English Costume in the Nineteenth Century, I. Brooke and J. Laver (Black)
A History of English Footwear, I. Brooke (Methuen)
English Costume 1900–1950, I. Brooke (Methuen)
English Costume 1066–1820, D. C. Calthrop (Black)
Costume of the Western World series, ed. J. Laver (Harrap)
Dress, J. Laver (Murray)
The Story of Clothes, A. Allen (Faber)
English Fashion, A. Settle (Collins)

Costume Cavalcade, H. H. Hansen (Methuen)
Everyday Costume in Britain, A. I. Barfoot (Batsford)
A Pictorial History of Costume, W. Bruhn and M. Tilke (Zwemmer)
A History of Everyday Things in England, 5 vols., M. and C. H. B. Quennell (Batsford)
Gallery of English Costume, published by the Art Galleries Committee, Manchester—eight small booklets
English Historic Costume Painting Books (Winsor & Newton)
English Costume: from the Second Century B.C. to 1960, D. Yarwood (Batsford)
Look at the Past, Part 3, Clothes, M. Schroeder (Chatto)—simple but some good ideas
Clothes, L. Fry (E.S.A.)
Hairstyles and Hairdressing, M. Harrison (Ward Lock)

Arms and Armour

A topic more likely to appeal to boys than to girls though it could be included in a study of costume or alternatively widened to cover medieval warfare. Again the chronological limits of the subject must be set after reading the relevant sections in a children's encyclopaedia or in one or two of the simple books listed first at the end of this section.

The main headings for a study of arms and armour might be:
1. The principles of armour involve a balance between:
   (a) Attack and defence. With the invention of each new weapon comes a new type of armour or defence.
   (b) The need to move (mobility) and safety (strength and weight).
2. Armour and weapons of the Greeks, Etruscans, Romans.
3. Introduction of the stirrup. Fully armoured man not so easily unseated. Horses armoured too.
4. Swords. Early weapons and metal workers; improvements. Viking sword.
5. Armour and weapons during Dark Ages and early Middle Ages.

Chain mail, helmets, etc. Evidence of Bayeux tapestry. Bows
and arrows. Padded garments.

6. Armour, weapons and the Crusades. Sleeveless surcoats.
7. Heraldry. Devices on shields, surcoats, horse trappings, etc.
8. Introduction of plate armour (thirteenth century). Changes in
   head protection.
9. Jousting and tournaments.
10. Fourteenth century. Transition from predominance of mail
    to that of plate armour. Increasing skill of armourer, com-
    plicated sections riveted to move with the body.
11. Fifteenth century. Italian armour, Gothic armour.
12. English archers of the fourteenth and fifteenth centuries. The
    long-bow and the cross-bow.
13. Sixteenth century. Fine decorated armour of Milan, etc. Ar-
    mour more like civilian dress.
14. Seventeenth century. Short, flat breast-plates, pot helmets, etc.
15. Gunpowder and the disappearance of armour.

Recommended Books

A Book of Armour, P. Nicolle (Puffin)
Arms and Armour in England, Sir James Mann (H.M.S.O.)
A Knight and His Armour; *A Knight and His Weapons*; *A Knight
    and His Horse*, R. E. Oakeshott (Lutterworth)
Arms and Armour, F. Wilkinson (Black)
European Armour, C. Blair (Batsford)
Monumental Brasses, Sir James Mann (King Penguin)
Church Brasses, A. C. Bouquet (Batsford)
The Archaeology of Weapons, R. E. Oakeshott (Lutterworth)
The Roman Army, G. Webster (Chester Museum)
Swords and Daggers, J. Hayward (Victoria & Albert Museum)
Arms and Armour in Tudor and Stuart London, M. Holmes (London
    Museum)
The Bayeux Tapestry, E. Maclagen (Penguin)
Sword, Lance and Bayonet, C. Foulkes (Cambridge)
Guns, S. E. Ellacott (Methuen)

The Story of the Gun, A. Wilson (Woolwich)
European Firearms, J. F. Hayward (H.M.S.O.)
The Tower of London (H.M.S.O.)

Warfare

If the last project is to include warfare through the ages or medieval warfare, many of the headings listed above will have to be dealt with in only a paragraph or so. The headings for a history of warfare might be:

1. The causes of warfare.
2. Early hand weapons. Early trained armies—Egyptian, Babylonian, Assyrian, Greek. Use of chariots.
3. The Roman Legions. Cavalry. The stirrup and saddle.
4. Medieval warfare. Knights and armour. Archers. Sieges and siege weapons. Castles.
5. Fourteenth century. The first guns. Effect on fortifications. Cannons and muskets.
6. Eighteenth century. Infantry and cavalry. Duke of Marlborough.
7. Napoleonic wars. Crimean War.
8. Railways. Larger, more mobile cannon. New weapons.
9. First World War. Trench warfare. Gas. Tanks. Aircraft.
10. Second World War. Mobility. Air attacks on civilians. Missiles.

Recommended Books

The Story of Land Warfare, P. Kendall (Hamish Hamilton)
Medieval English Warfare, R. R. Sellman (Methuen)
Look at Castles, A. Duggan (Hamish Hamilton)
Castles and Fortresses, R. R. Sellman (Methuen)
The Medieval Castle, M. E. Reeves (Longmans)
Soldiers and Sailors, N. Wymer (Oxford)—Marlborough, Wolfe, Wellington, Gordon and Clive
Discovering the Army, D. Scott Daniell (U.L.P.)
The Army, E. W. Gladstone (Blackwell)

The First World War; *The Second World War*, R. R. Sellman
(Methuen)
World War I and *World War II*, D. Scott Daniell (Benn)
The True Book of the British Army; *The True Book of the Royal Navy*;
The True Book of the Royal Air Force (Muller)
The Wonder Book of the Army; *The Wonder Book of the Navy*; *The
Wonder Book of the Air Force* (Ward Lock)
The Second World War, J. M. Selby (Allen & Unwin)

Museums, galleries, etc.

Belfast, Museum and Art Gallery
Birmingham, City Museum and Art Gallery
Bristol, City Museum
Cambridge, Fitzwilliam Museum
Canterbury, Westgate Museum
Chester, Grosvenor Museum
Edinburgh, Scottish United Services Museum
Glasgow, Art Gallery and Museum
Hatfield House, Hertfordshire
Maidstone, Museum and Art Gallery
Leeds, Abbey House.
Lincoln, City and County Museum
London—British Museum, Imperial War Museum, Tower of
London, Victoria & Albert, Wallace Collection, Hampton Court
Newcastle-on-Tyne, Laing Art Gallery and Museum
Sheffield Park Museum, Sussex
Warwick Castle Museum
York Castle Museum

The Russian Revolution
or Modern Russia

The pupil who likes his history reasonably up-to-date or is interested in current events and politics may find this an attractive

topic. The first step should probably be to read an account of the Russian Revolution in a good encyclopaedia or in a history text-book such as *Britain's Place in the World*, Book IV, by L. F. Hobley (Oliver & Boyd) and to jot down the main headings under which the story can be told. The encyclopaedias should also be consulted under the names of Marx, Lenin, Trotsky, Stalin, etc. The pupil can then decide how much background he wants to put in. A comprehensive plan from which the teacher can make suggestions to the pupil is as follows (items 2–5 or 6 need only be a paragraph or so each):

1. Map of U.S.S.R. with scale showing its immense size. Mention of different peoples of Russia.

2. Description of Russia in nineteenth century. Four-fifths of the population were peasants, tied to the land until 1851; they were then freed but few were able to buy their own land. Hard, miserable lives. Industrialization begins, but low wages, slums, no trade unions allowed, etc.

3. Portrait of Czar Nicholas II (1894–1917), weak, obstinate, believer in Divine Right.

4. 1904–5, Russo–Japanese War, Russians defeated. Unrest, strikes, march on Winter Palace, St Petersburg attacked by Cossacks—'Bloody Sunday'. Czar promised parliamentary reform but ineffective. Bolshevik Communists building up underground movement; leader Lenin in exile.

5. Influence of Rasputin on Empress and Czar, and fate of Rasputin.

6. World War I. Russia entered war in 1914 allied with France and England against Germany and Austria-Hungary. Early successes, then defeats and great loss of life because ill-equipped and led. Mass desertions.

7. Revolution of March 1917. Czar abdicated. Provisional Government headed by Prince Lvov. Tries to keep Russia in war; more riots and strikes.

8. The Revolutionary Parties: (1) Social Revolutionaries—party of peasants willing to support Provisional Government if introducing sweeping reforms; (2) Social Democrats—followers of Karl Marx who believed in the class struggle of the workers

against the upper classes. Brief account here of ideas and influence of Karl Marx. In 1903 the Social Democrats split into two groups: (a) the Mensheviks (so-called 'minority' group), whose leader, Alexander Kerensky, became Prime Minister of the Provisional Government; and (b) the Bolsheviks ('majority' group), later called the Communists, who opposed the Provisional Government and aimed at seizing power themselves. In March 1917 they urged soldiers and sailors to ignore the orders of the Provisional Government.

9. Leaders of the Revolution—Lenin, Trotsky. Brief account of their lives up to 1917.

10. Revolution of October/November 1917 led by Lenin and Trotsky. Escape of Kerensky, little bloodshed. Council of People's Commissars set up. Peace made with Germany. Civil War 1917–1920 between the Reds (Communists) and the Whites (monarchists). European intervention to help Whites. Murder of Czar and family.

11. Reorganization of Russia into Union of Soviet Socialist Republics. Four, later 12, and later still 16 states. Organization of the soviets. The rôle of the Communist Party.

12. The new economic policy 1921–1928.

13. Death of Lenin, 1924. Struggle for leadership. Trotsky's flight to Mexico. The rise of Stalin.

14. The Five Year Plans, 1928–1933, 1933–1938 and 1938–1942.

15. Soviet Russia in World War II. Soviet Pact with Hitler's Germany, August 1939. Germany and Russia divide up Poland. In June 1941 Germany attacks Russia, Russia becomes ally of Britain. Defence of Moscow. Siege of Stalingrad. Russia's great damage and losses in War.

16. After World War II many countries with support of U.S.S.R. become Communist—Poland, Rumania, Czechoslovakia, Albania, Hungary and East Germany. Known as the 'Communist bloc'. Development of 'cold war' between Communist bloc and former allies because of fear of spread of Communism. 'Iron Curtain'.

17. Death of Stalin. Account of his life and influence. New struggle

for power. Malenkov, Bulganin, Khrushchev, 'Destalinization'.
Fall of Khrushchev. Leadership today.
18. Russia's place in the modern world. Space race. Russia and
United Nations, etc.

Recommended Books

A Visual History of Russia, J. D. Reid (Evans)
The First Book of the Soviet Union, L. L. Snyder (Edmund Ward)
Meet Soviet Russia, J. Gunter (Hamish Hamilton)
The Story of Russia, A. Earl (U.L.P.)
Introducing the U.S.S.R., B. King (Pitman)
Inside Russia Today, J. Gunter (Hamish Hamilton)
Russia, the Land and the People, J. Charnock (Bodley Head)
The True Book about the Russian Revolution, J. Fisher (Muller)
People and Power, K. Savage (Oxford)
Ten Days that Shook the World, J. Reed (Penguin)
They Made History, Volume 3, H. Bellis (Cassell)—on Lenin
Russia and Her People, A. Nazaroff (Lutterworth)
Russia, J. Lawrence (Methuen)
Soviet Russia, J. Lawrence (Benn)
Russia: Lenin and Stalin, D. G. Fry (Hamish Hamilton)
Russia, B. Hammond (Blond Educational)
The Cold War, D. Heater (Oxford)
Russia under the Tsars, H. Moscow (Cassell)
Karl Marx and Our Times, K. W. Watkins (Hamish Hamilton)
The Growth of Modern Russia, J. Kennett (Blackie)
Twentieth-Century Russia, S. Pickering (Oxford)
The Russian Revolution, A. Cash (Jackdaw, Cape)

World Organizations

A suitable topic for the child who likes his history as up-to-date as
possible or who is interested in politics, current affairs, peace organizations or world health and hunger problems. Sometimes such
a child may be emotionally committed to a point of view without

much real information to back it up, so that a study of the background to the immediate issues may be useful and illuminating.

The first step should be to read one or more accounts of world or international co-operation and organizations in a junior or other encyclopaedia and a simple account of the United Nations Organization and the League of Nations. A skeleton plan might then be prepared, and some decision taken about the limits of the project. Some children may enjoy investigating the early ideas on world organizations and analysing the success and failures of the League of Nations in detail, while others will prefer to dismiss items 1–7 below in a few brief paragraphs and start on item 8. A comprehensive plan might include:

1. Early attempts, or views about how to outlaw war by international agreement: the Greeks; fifteenth century—George Podiebrad, King of Bohemia; sixteenth and seventeenth centuries—Duc de Sully, Hugo Grotius, William Penn; eighteenth century—Rousseau; nineteenth century—Concert of Europe, Kant.

2. First serious attempt to set up machinery to maintain world peace was the establishment of the League of Nations in 1920. The spirit of the Treaty of Versailles and its effect on the League of Nations. President Wilson's Fourteen Points.

3. The structure of the League. The Covenant, the Assembly, the Secretariat, the International Labour Office, the Court of International Justice.

4. The aims of the League. Prevention of war by submitting quarrels to international arbitration. Reduction of armaments.

5. The League's work for people in distress. Refugees and prisoners-of-war, world health, slavery, working conditions, etc.

6. Successes of the League in preventing war: Sweden and Finland, 1920; Yugoslavia and Albania, 1921; Greece and Italy, 1923; Greco-Bulgarian dispute, 1925.

7. The League in difficulties: (a) Germany, (b) Japanese aggression in China from 1931, (c) Italian attack on Abyssinia in 1935, (d) German troops in Rhineland in 1936, (e) Spanish Civil War, 1936.

8. During the Second World War the nations were already thinking about how to secure a permanent peace. Atlantic Charter, August 1941: public pledge of U.S.A. and U.K. to ultimate freedom. Dumbarton Oaks, 1944. San Francisco Conference, 1945, to draw up plans for a United Nations Organization.

9. United Nations Charter. Quote from Preamble. Six main organs of United Nations and explanation of their functions— General Assembly, Security Council, Economic and Social Council, Secretariat, International Court of Justice, Trusteeship Council. United Nations Budget.

10. United Nations Assembly Declaration of Human Rights. The history of the struggle for the rights of man by many nations could be mentioned briefly here as background if wished— Magna Carta, Habeas Corpus, United States Declaration of Independence, French Rights of Man, abolition of slavery, right to vote, etc.

11. United Nations Economic and Social Council ('Welfare Council'), helping children in need (UNICEF), helping refugees (UNRRA), under-developed countries/disease (WHO), illiteracy (UNESCO), food supplies (FAO), working conditions (ILO), economic aid, loans, etc. Other agencies, e.g. Universal Postal Union, meteorological services, technical aid schemes.

12. The problem of keeping peace. The Security Council's successes and failures. Indonesian Dispute in 1947. War between Jews and Arabs in Palestine in 1948. Korea, 1950–1953. Suez Crisis, 1956. Hungary, 1956. The Congo, 1960–2.

13. Some problems for the United Nations: disunity of Great Powers; use of veto in Security Council; membership of Communist China; finances.

Recommended Books

United Nations for the Classroom, G. J. Jones and E. T. Davis (Routledge)
The United Nations, J. Hornby (Macmillan)
This is the United Nations, H. Spaull (Rockliff)—very simple

The First Book of the United Nations, E. Epstein (Mayflower)
The Story of the United Nations, K. Savage (Bodley Head)
The United Nations, K. Savage (Blond Educational)
The United Nations at Work, G. T. Hankin (H.M.S.O.)
The World Unites Against Want, H. Spaull (Rockliff)
Living in Communities, Book 3, 'Our World Community', P. B. Hilton and A. L. Toothill (Macmillan)
The United Nations and What You Should Know About It (United Nations)—very simple
The United Nations, J. Kennett (Blackie)
Basic Facts about the United Nations (United Nations)
A History of Europe from the Eighteenth Century to 1937, H. A. L. Fisher (Eyre & Spottiswoode)—especially Chapter XCVIII.
Britain's Place in the World, Book 4, L. F. Hobley (Oliver & Boyd)

Sources of Information

Council for Education in World Citizenship, United Nations Association—25 Charles Street, London W.I

United Nations Information Centre, 14–15 Stratford Place, London W.I

UNESCO Headquarters, Place de Fontenoy, Paris 7e

Exploration, Voyages of Discovery, Map-makers

An enormous subject from which the pupil must attempt a brief general survey or must select a section for special and more detailed study. This topic is suitable for children who enjoy the dramatic and adventurous aspects of history and for those who are good at geography and map-drawing. It can be done either more or less chronologically, or by selecting particular fields of exploration, e.g. the Antarctic, Africa, underwater, etc., or by linking the lives of individual great explorers.

First the child must read a simple account of exploration such as *The World is Round* by F. Debenham (Rathbone), *They Went Exploring* by R. S. Lambert (Schofield & Sims) or *A Book of Discovery* by M. B. Synge (Nelson), or look up explorers and exploration in one of the good children's encyclopaedias. Then he should decide on the chronological or subject limits of the project and prepare a plan of headings or chapters.

Here are some possible headings from which a selection can be made:

1. Early explorers. The Egyptians, Cretans, Phoenicians and Greeks. Circumnavigation of Africa. The Persians. Xenophon, Alexander the Great.

2. The Romans. Exploration and military conquest: Britain, the East, Africa.

3. Early map-makers. Eratosthenes, 200 B.C., realized that the earth is a sphere and made a reasonable calculation of its size. Ptolemy: latitude and longitude.

4. Early Christian missionaries: St Patrick, St Columba.

5. Viking exploration. Shetland and Faroe Islands, the Orkneys, Hebrides, Greenland and North American Coast, Vinland and the Vinland map.

6. Moslem exploration and conquest in seventh and eighth centuries A.D.

7. Seventh century A.D. Chinese exploration and trade routes.

8. The flat world. Maps in the Dark Ages.

9. Thirteenth century. The Mongol Empire. Ghenghis Khan. Marco Polo. Voyages to China. Ibn Battuta—Moslem explorer of Asia and Africa.

10. The Great Age of Discovery in the fifteenth century. Exploration from Europe eastwards.

  A. *The Portuguese*: Overland routes to East made difficult by the successes of the Turks (fall of Constantinople, 1453). Search for alternative sea route. Prince Henry the Navigator: encouragement of trade, exploration of African coast, development of ships and navigational instruments. Cadamosto, Fernan Gomez, Diego Cam. Bartholomew Diaz rounds the Cape of Good Hope. Vasco da Gama reaches India.

B. *The Spanish*: A westward route to the east. Christopher Columbus reaches West Indies and mainland of South America. Amerigo Vespucci. Spanish Conquest of Mexico and exploration of South America. Balboa, Cortez, Pizarro.

11. John Cabot: more northerly route across Atlantic, Newfoundland, Greenland. Sebastian Cabot: Nova Scotia, Hudson Bay and later across south Atlantic and to South America.

12. Ferdinand Magellan, first circumnavigation of the earth.

13. Sixteenth century. Exploration of South America. Establishment of Spanish influence in West Indies. Amerigo Vespucci, Pizarro, Balboa, Cortez. Legend of El Dorado.

14. The search for the North-West Passage. Jacques Cartier, Sir Humphrey Gilbert, Martin Frobisher, John Davis, Henry Hudson, William Baffin. Colonization of east coast of America. Overland expeditions into interior.

15. Some explorers in Asia. The search for the North-East Passage—Richard Chancellor, Anthony Jenkinson, Willem Barents.

16. The exploration of Australasia. Early Portuguese and Spanish landings in East Indies. Dutch discoveries and settlements in East Indies. Van Dieman, Tasman, Captain Cook.

17. The exploration of Africa. Early slave traders. Missions from Europe to Christian Ethiopia and the legend of Prester John. Missionary explorers. James Bruce, Mungo Park, Burton and Speke, Livingstone and Stanley.

18. Exploration of polar regions. Early exploration of Arctic regions when searching for North-West and North-East Passages to India. John Ross, James Clark Ross, Edward Parry, John Franklin. The struggle to reach the North Pole—Nansen, Amundsen, Peary. Early exploration of the Antarctic—James Clark Ross. Captain Robert Scott and Amundsen race for Pole. Fuchs and Hillary.

19. Exploration under the sea.
20. Exploring mountains, crossing unknown deserts, etc. Everest.
21. Space exploration. Man now planning to leave his planet. Early rockets. First Sputnik, October 1957. Man in space.

Recommended Books

General

Discovery and Exploration, F. Debenham (Hamlyn)
Exploration and Adventure, C. Collinson (Allen & Unwin)
They Put Out to Sea, R. Duvoisin (U.L.P.)
Exploring the Pacific; *Opening Africa*; *Early Explorers*; and *Exploring the Americas*, L. F. Hobley (Methuen)
Unrolling the Map: the Story of Exploration, L. Outhwaite (Constable)
Vast Horizons: a Story of True Adventure and Discovery, M. S. Lucas (Harrap)
Beyond the Sunset: a Book of Explorers, E. J. Boog-Watson and J. I. Carruthers (Oxford)
A History of Exploration, Sir Percy Sykes (Routledge)
A Book of Discovery, M. B. Synge (Nelson)
Great Navigators and Discoveries, J. A. Brendon (Harrap)—24 explorers from Hanno to Franklin
The Boy's Book of Exploration, ed. Sir Edmund Hillary (Cassell)
The Romance of Navigation, W. B. Whall (Sampson Low)
The Story of Ships, S. E. Ellacott (Methuen)
A Picture History of Great Discoveries, M. E. George (Oxford)
How the World Was Explored, M. Neurath and J. A. Lauwerys (Parrish)
The Real Book about Explorers, I. Block (Dobson)
The Eagle Book of Modern Adventurers (Hulton)
The Elizabethan Seamen, R. R. Sellman (Methuen)
The Westward Crossings, J. Mirsky (Knopf)
Explorers and Exploration, D. Scott Daniell (Batsford)
Explorers All, C. Collinson (Hutchinson)

The Study Book of Maps, R. S. Barker (Bodley Head)
Mapping the World, E. Raisz (Abelard-Schuman)
Exploring Maps, P. Moore and H. Brinton (Odhams)—very simple
Voyages of the Great Discoverers, E. Wood (Harrap)
Exploration of Africa, T. Sterling (Cassell)

Collective Biographies

Six Great Explorers, D. Divine (Hamish Hamilton)—Frobisher, Cook, Park, Burton, Livingstone, Scott
Six Explorers, J. Walton (Oxford)—Polo, Columbus, Cook, Sturt, Livingstone, Scott
Six More Explorers, J. Walton (Oxford)—Magellan, da Gama, Cartier, Park, Burton, Amundsen
Great Explorers, N. Wymer (Oxford)—Columbus, Magellan, Cook, Mackenzie, Franklin, Livingstone, Scott, Hunt.

Individual Biographies

Marco Polo, M. Komroff (Methuen)
Marco Polo, M. Collis (Faber)
He Went with Marco Polo; *He Went with Christopher Columbus*; *He Went with Vasco da Gama*, L. A. Kent (Harrap)—story form
Christopher Columbus and *The Voyages of Captain Cook*, J. Langdon-Davies (Jackdaw, Jonathan Cape)
The Log of Christopher Columbus's First Voyage, J. O. H. Cosgrave (W. H. Allen)
The Real Book of Christopher Columbus, I. Block (Dobson)
Over the Edge of the World: the Story of Henry the Navigator, I. L. Plunket (Lutterworth)
Ferdinand Magellan, W. Welch (Oxford)
All About Captain Cook, A. Sperry (W. H. Allen)
Captain James Cook, J. Merrett (Muller)
Captain Cook, C. Lloyd (Faber)
Captain Cook and the South Pacific, O. Warner (Cassell)

The North and South Poles

The North Pole, E. Shipton (Muller)
The South Pole, G. F. Lamb (Muller)
Discovery of the Poles, Q. Riley and R. Taylor (Puffin)
The Polar Explorer, E. W. K. Walton (E.S.A.)
Heroes of Polar Exploration, R. Andrist (Cassell)
Nansen, A. de Selincourt (Oxford)
Fridtjof Nansen, F. Noel-Baker (Black)
The Long White Road, M. H. Albert (Lutterworth)—Shackleton
South with Shackleton, M. E. Carter (Longmans)
Captain Scott, M. E. Carter (Longmans)
Scott of the Antarctic, B. Webster Smith (Blackie)
Scott's Last Expedition, extracts from his journals (Murray)
South with Scott, Admiral Lord Mountevans (Collins)
Antarctic Adventure, Sir Vivian Fuchs (Cassell)

Undersea Exploration

Undersea Explorer, J. Dugan (Hamish Hamilton)—Captain Cousteau
The Silent World, J.-Y. Cousteau (Hamish Hamilton)
Man Explores the Sea, J. Dugan (Hamish Hamilton)

Museums

Scott Polar Research Institute, Cambridge
Scottish Memorial to David Livingstone, Blantyre, Lanarkshire, Scotland
National Maritime Museum, Greenwich, London S.E.10
Science Museum, South Kensington, London S.W.7
Museum of Literary and Philosophical Society, Whitby, Yorkshire (for Captain Cook)
Buckland Abbey and Tythe Barn, Plymouth (for Sir Francis Drake)
Royal Geographical Society Museum, 1 Kensington Gore, London W.8

Homes, Castles, Churches

This is an extremely wide and well-documented field from which the pupil should select the aspects which interest him most. He would probably be well advised to select either the history of houses or of church architecture or of castles for a long period or to restrict himself to a limited period for all kinds of building, e.g. medieval building, Tudor architecture, etc. Alternatively he could choose to write a history of different features in building through the ages, e.g. building materials, windows, doors, heating, lighting, cooking facilities, etc. This is clearly a topic for the child who enjoys drawing and gives a chance to the artistic pupil less able at writing to do valuable but largely visual work. For convenience, I have divided this field into three sections. In any of these studies it might be a good idea for the pupil to provide a glossary of technical terms which are used in the account and which need not then be explained or defined each time they crop up. This is especially necessary in the case of church-building with such words as clerestory, corbel, lancet, piscina, reredos, squint, etc., and in the case of castles where it may be easier to use the terms machicolation, merlon, embrasure, vallum, fosse, etc., without explaining their meaning constantly.

First the pupil should be encouraged to browse through several general introductory books about building in order to set the limits of his study. Such books as *Your Local Buildings* by K. Harston and E. Davis (Allen & Unwin), *The Story of English Architecture* by H. Braun (Faber) or *Your Book of Architecture* by A. and J. Allen (Faber) would do well for a start. Then, having decided on what aspects of this enormous subject to specialize in, the pupil should sketch the main headings for his study. For the skeleton plans I have made the most obvious division in types of building:

A. HOMES

1. Old Stone Age homes—caves, the first huts, camps.
2. New Stone Age homes—pit dwellings, wattle and daub huts.

3. The Bronze and Iron Ages—lake villages, beehive huts.
4. Roman houses and towns. Villas, town houses, baths, central heating, mosaic pavements.
5. Saxon cruck dwellings. The Saxon village.
6. Homes in the early Middle Ages. Norman Castles—motte and bailey, and square towers. Manor houses. Peasants' homes. Town houses.
7. Later Middle Ages. Improvements in manor houses, glass windows, more privacy. Half-timbering and plaster.
8. Tudor houses. Manor houses, town houses, ordinary houses. Improved timber frames. Brickwork.
9. Jacobean and Stuart houses. Inigo Jones and Grinling Gibbons. Classical influences.
10. Queen Anne and Georgian houses. The Age of Elegance. The Regency style. Robert Adam, John Nash.
11. Victorian period. Gothic revival. Influence of William Morris. Effects of industrialization—slums, back-to-back houses, etc.
12. Twentieth century. Ribbon development. Suburbia. Flats. Town Planning. New towns.

There is also the possibility in this topic, if a child flags in his enthusiasm for buildings, to extend the study to the inside of the home—furniture, clothes, kitchens and food, plumbing and sanitation, gardens—and perhaps to make the time-span shorter than originally intended.

Recommended Books

Homes, M. Harrison (E.S.A.)
Discovering Houses, W. Earnshaw (U.L.P.)
Your Hearth and Home, E. E. H. Guest (Allen & Unwin)
Houses, L. Cowie (Cassell)
Home Life, T. Hastie (Batsford)
Town Life, S. Healy (Batsford)
The Englishman Builds, R. Tubbs (Penguin)
A Study Book of Houses, C. Warburton (Bodley Head)—very simple
Let's Look at Houses and Homes, J. Morey (Muller)

Our Own Homes Through the Ages, P. Moss (Harrap)
The Story of Your Home, A. Miller (Faber)
How to Look at Old Buildings, E. Vale (Batsford)
The Miniature History of the English House (Architectural Press)
Houses and *Interiors*, M. and A. Potter (Murray)
The Englishman's Castle, J. Gloag (Eyre & Spottiswoode)
The English Home, D. Yarwood (Batsford)
The English Country House, R. Dutton (Batsford)
The English Cottage, H. Batsford and C. Fry (Batsford)
National Trust Buildings, J. Lees Milne (Batsford)
Mr Budge Builds a House, G. Anderson (Brockhampton)—simple
    but amusing
Exploring Old Buildings, E. V. Clark (Hollis & Carter)
Architecture for Children, J. and M. Fry (Allen & Unwin)
History in Pictures, Bk. 1 Houses, E. J. Boog-Watson and J. I. Car-
    ruthers (Oxford)—very good time-chart and illustrations
The Observer's Book of Architecture, J. Penoyre and M. Ryan
    (Warne)
Historical Houses of Great Britain, H. and R. Leacroft (Puffin)
Towns and *Houses*, E. Osmond (Batsford, Junior Heritage Series)
Evidence in Pictures, I. Doncaster (Longmans)
On the Track of the Past, F. W. Robins (Phoenix House)
A History of Houses, R. J. Unstead (Black)
An Introduction to Social History, C. R. Wright (Associated News-
    papers)
Your Local Buildings, K. Harston and E. Davis (Allen & Unwin)
The Architecture of England, F. Gibberd (Architectural Press)
A Sense of History, Book I, J. S. M. Smith (Edward Arnold)
The Medieval Village and *The Medieval Town*, M. E. Reeve (Long-
    mans)
Building and Shelter, C. F. G. Viner (Longmans)
Your Book of Architecture, A. and J. Allen (Faber)
A First Book of Architecture and *A Second Book of Architecture*,
    G. H. Reed (Black)
The Story of English Architecture, H. Brown (Faber)
A Little Book of Architecture, N. Jewson (Oxford)

B. CASTLES

1. Early defences against attack. Earthworks, forts and camps.
2. Roman fortifications.
3. The first real castles—motte and bailey castles. Examples and drawings.
4. Norman stone castles of the twelfth century. Square keeps: Tower of London, Colchester, Canterbury, Castle Rising, Kenilworth. Circular or shell keeps: Arundel, Lewes, Tamworth, etc. Keeps in baileys.
5. Methods of defending castles. Development of curtain walls, wall towers, barbicans. The draw-bridge and portcullis. Arrow loops, machicolation, merlons.
6. Methods of attacking castles: siege towers and engines, mining and sapping, scaling ladders, mantlets, catapults, trebuchets, mangonels, etc.
7. Life inside a medieval castle. Private household quarters, soldiers' quarters, servants' quarters, stables, stores, workshops, kitchens, etc.
8. Influence of the Crusaders on British castles—Krak de Chevaliers, etc. Development of concentric castles, e.g. Caerphilly and Edward I's castles—Conway, Caernarvon, Beaumaris and Harlech. Moated castles, e.g. Bodiam, Hurstmonceux. Castles without keeps.
9. Fourteenth century. Invention of the cannon. Decline of castles. Fortified manor houses, peel towers.

Recommended Books

Castles and Fortresses, R. R. Sellman (Methuen)
Castles, L. Fry (E.S.A.)
Exploring Castles, W. D. Simpson (Routledge)
Look at Castles, A. Duggan (Hamish Hamilton)
The Medieval Castle, M. E. Reeves (Longmans)
English Castles, R. A. Brown (Batsford)
The True Book about Castles, H. Treece (Muller)

Discovering Castles, W. Earnshaw (U.L.P.)
The Gauntlet, Ronald Welch (Oxford)—fiction
The Mad Miller of Wareham, Joyce Reason (Oxford)—fiction; set in
Corfe Castle

C. CHURCH ARCHITECTURE

1. Christianity reintroduced to Britain in the seventh century A.D.,
   and Saxons began to build churches. Most of these destroyed
   by heathen Danes but a few whole and many part buildings remain. Small windows and doors, triangular arches.
2. Norman or Romanesque, 1066–1200. Massiveness, roundness.
   Round arches and windows, dark, thick cylindrical columns,
   chevron patterns, barrel vaulting, squat square towers: e.g.
   Durham Cathedral; Winchester Cathedral; Temple Church,
   London; chapel, Ludlow Castle; Chapel of Tower of London,
   etc.
3. Early English, earliest phase of 'Gothic' style, 1200–1300.
   Pointed arches, flying buttresses, higher, lighter churches. Tall,
   thin windows, lancet windows.
4. Decorated period, 1300–1400. Simplicity of thirteenth century
   replaced by highly decorated style. General architectural principles similar to previous century but ornate tracery, stained
   glass, intricate carving in vaulting, on columns, etc.
5. Perpendicular period, 1400–1500. Improved building methods
   led to thinner walls, height and light. Simplicity, austerity. Flat-
   ter arches, larger windows, improved vaulting. Hammer-beam
   roof.
6. Little church-building in Tudor period because of upheavals
   following breakaway from Roman Catholic Church, nor in first
   three-quarters of seventeenth century—social and religious
   upheavals. Great amount of rebuilding of churches of London
   after the Great Fire of 1666. Influence of Renaissance on
   Church architecture—classical proportions, influence of Pal-
   ladio. Christopher Wren's city churches and St Paul's Cathedral.
   Eighteenth century—Wren's principles continued by Vanbrugh
   and Hawksmoor.

7. Nineteenth century. Gothic revival. New materials.
8. Twentieth century. Recent developments. Modern churches.

Recommended Books

Look at Churches, A. Duggan (Hamish Hamilton)
Churches, K. A. Lindley (E.S.A.)
The Observer's Book of Architecture, J. Penoyre and M. Ryan (Warne)
The Parish Church, P. Thornhill (Methuen)
A Third Book of Architecture, G. H. Reed (Black)
Churches and Cathedrals, H. and R. Leacroft (Puffin)
English Churches, R. R. Sellman (Methuen)
Churches and *Cathedrals*, E. Vale (Batsford)
Guide books to cathedrals, churches, abbeys, etc., many published by H.M.S.O.
Westminster Abbey, C. Clair (Bruce & Cawthorn)

Also guide books to individual houses (National Trust Series and English Life publications) and guides to Ministry of Works properties.

Visits

With this topic, of course, the opportunities for making visits to suitable houses, castles or churches are innumerable. Three useful publications listing places of interest and when they can be visited are—

The National Trust List of Properties
Country Houses Open to the Public
Historic Houses and Castles Open to the Public

There are also a large number of museums that have collections of furniture and other household items. Notable ones are the Castle Museum, York; the Victoria and Albert Museum, London S.W.7; the Geffrye Museum, London E.1. A complete list of museums and their special collections can be found in *Museums and Galleries in Great Britain and Ireland* (Index Publications Ltd).

Education and Schools

Very few books exclusively on this subject have been written for children or young people. Material has to be gathered, therefore, from the chapters on education, or even odd paragraphs discovered by using the index, in several social history books. The first step should be to read a brief history of education in one of the encyclopaedias and to decide on the limits to be set in the proposed study. Headings or a skeleton plan of the work should be put together. Probably most young people will want to restrict their studies to a history of schools for children rather than also to cover the education of adults in colleges and universities. Most children, too, will be more interested in comparatively modern developments, over the last 150 years or so. In the specimen plan below, however, the whole range of headings is covered from which a selection can be made.

1. Schools in the ancient civilizations. Sumerian schools. Cuneiform writing on tablets. Arithmetic, etc.
2. Indian and Chinese civilizations. Ancient Egypt and Persia.
3. Schools in Ancient Greece. Plato's discussion of education. The Spartan view. Gymnastics, artistic pursuits.
4. Jewish education. Synagogue schools.
5. The education of a Roman boy.
6. The Dark Ages in Europe, little respect for education. Arab learning.

Most children will probably prefer to write only a paragraph or two as background introduction to their work on headings 1–6 above, or even to start completely from item 7.

7. Education in the Middle Ages. The training of sons of the nobility in chivalry and the arts of war. Chantry or Song Schools

attached to monasteries. Schools run or private lessons given by parish priests. Early grammar schools.

8. More grammar schools founded after Reformation with money from dissolved monasteries. Grammar school curriculum—mainly Latin, rhetoric, logic. After Renaissance, Greek also studied. Tradition of classical studies as the basis of secondary and university education has remained until fairly recent times.

9. New ideas on the content of education. John Locke.

This is another possible starting point for those who do not want to go into the comparatively limited education of a privileged few but prefer to begin with the early steps towards state education in the nineteenth century.

10. Schools in existence in the eighteenth and early nineteenth centuries: (a) Charity Schools, (b) Grammar Schools, (c) Public Schools, (d) Dames' Schools, (e) Sunday Schools. Robert Raikes.

11. First intervention of Government in education. 1802 Health and Morals of Apprentices Act—compulsory part-time instruction for pauper apprentices in factories.

12. Schools in the early years of the nineteenth century. The work of the National Society and the British and Foreign Schools Society. Joseph Lancaster and Andrew Bell. The monitorial system. First Government grant for education, 1833.

13. Special committee of the Privy Council, 1839. Appointment of Inspectors. Standards of elementary education. Religious divisions. Newcastle Commission, 1858. Robert Lowe and 'Payment by Results'.

14. 1867 Reform Act gives vote to working men in towns. Need to educate 'our masters'. 1870, Forster's Education Act. Beginning of State education. Dual system of voluntary and School Board schools. Non-denominational religious teaching in State schools from which parents could have children excluded if they wished. 1876, compulsory attendance at school from 5 to 10, though half-timers allowed. Mundella's Act, 1886, restricted child labour. 1891, all elementary schools made free. 1893, school-leaving age raised to 11.

15. 1899, establishment of Board of Education. 1902 Education

Act abolished School Boards and established Local Education Authorities to control elementary education both in voluntary and State schools, also secondary and technical schools.

16. The Public Schools—meaning 'independent schools'. Early public schools: King's School, Canterbury; St Peter's, York, seventh century; Winchester, 1394; Eton, 1443; etc. Connection with Church. Seventeenth and eighteenth centuries, public schools in bad repute. Nineteenth-century revival, reforms of Arnold of Rugby, Butler of Shrewsbury, etc., and new demand for boarding-school education from industrialists and merchants. Several new public schools. Public Schools Act, 1868. Girls' public schools. Fleming Report, 1942. Recent proposals to integrate public schools into State system.

17. Secondary schools. At first State participation in education restricted to elementary schools. Secondary education available for fee-payers in the endowed grammar schools, which also gave a few free places to poor scholars. 1895, Bryce Commission report on secondary schools. 1902 Education Act allowed Local Education Authorities to assist and control secondary schools. 1907 Act aided secondary schools to provide at least one-quarter free places. By 1914, six per cent of elementary school pupils go on to secondary schools. Effect of free-place examination on elementary schools. Growth of secondary schools between the wars. The Spens Report, 1938. Education Act, 1944. Secondary education for all, with 'parity of esteem' between grammar, technical and modern school. Eleven-plus examination. Comprehensive schools.

18. Technical education. Mid-nineteenth-century Mechanics' Institutes. The Polytechnics. Tendency to view technical education as suitable for adult evening classes. Limited development of technical high schools between the wars. The Spens Report. 1944 Act; secondary technical schools with 'parity of esteem'. Recent developments.

19. The 1918 Education Act (Fisher Act) raised school leaving age to 14. Distinguished between junior and senior education. The Hadow Report and reorganization.

20. Education during the Second World War. Evacuation. Air-raid precautions.
21. Education Act, 1944, and after.
Other headings that could be included are:
22. Nursery schools and classes.
23. Teachers. Training colleges.
24. School meals and milk. School medical service.
25. Universities.

Recommended Books

This England, 1714-1960, I. Tenen (Macmillan)
A Social and Economic History of Britain, P. Gregg (Harrap)—chapter on education
British Economic and Social History, C. P. Hill (Edward Arnold)
Social and Industrial History of England, F. W. Tickner (Edward Arnold)
The Georgian Child and *The Victorian Child*, F. G. Roe (Phoenix House)—chapter in each on 'School'
The Age of Reform, E. Garrett (Black)—chapter on Arnold of Rugby
A History of English Education from 1760, H. C. Barnard (U.L.P.)
Education in Britain, M. E. Hutchinson (Hamish Hamilton)
Picture Source Books for Social History, M. Harrison and A. A. M. Wells (Allen & Unwin)—all have pictures and extracts from contemporary sources on schools, teachers, etc.
A London Child of the Seventies, M. V. Hughes (Oxford)—chapter on schooldays
Charles Dickens and Early Victorian England, R. J. Cruikshank (Pitman)—chapter 9, and charts on literacy, etc.
A History of Everyday Things in England, M. and C. H. B. Quennell (Batsford)
The Day Before Yesterday, ed. N. Streatfeild (Collins)—chapter on school
Education, M. Seaborne (Studio Vista)
Schools, J. Howard Brown (Blackwell)

Learning and Teaching in Victorian Times, P. F. Speed (Longmans)
Illustrated English Social History, G. M. Trevelyan (Longmans)—
rather difficult but useful snippets can be gathered by using the
index
Education in England, W. K. Richmond (Pelican)—not written for
children but useful for clarifying facts glossed over in easier books

Fiction

Tom Brown's Schooldays, Thomas Hughes (Dent)
Nicholas Nickleby and *David Copperfield*, Charles Dickens (Everyman and many editions)

Useful Addresses

Department of Education and Science, Curzon Street, London w.1
National Union of Teachers, Hamilton House, Mabledon Place,
London w.c.1
Nursery School Association of Great Britain and Northern Ireland,
89 Stamford Street, London s.e.1

Farming and Country Life

The enthusiastic country child or the town child with a nostalgia
for country life might choose this topic. It is best to start the pupil
off with a simple general book such as *Country Life Through the
Ages* by E. Boog-Watson and J. I. Carruthers (Allen & Unwin) or
The Story of Agriculture by E. W. Burbridge (Pitman), or alternatively the teacher could suggest that the child consults one or two
encyclopaedias or economic history textbooks to get an overall picture of the subject. The next stage is to prepare a skeleton of the
history of farming so that the pupil can decide how far back and how
far up-to-date he wants to go in his study. Then he should plan his
chapter or section headings and the teacher can help by making
additional suggestions and discussing suitable limits of the project.

A reasonable plan for the history of British farming might be as follows:

1. The first farmers. Early farming tools and domestic animals.
2. Roman farming in Britain.
3. Anglo-Saxon farming. The open-field strip system. Organization of work.
4. The feudal system. Life on the medieval manor.
5. Break-up of the manorial system. Rent instead of services. The Black Death. The Peasants' Revolt.
6. Sheep rearing. Enclosures in the sixteenth century.

Alternatively 1–6 could be covered in a section entitled 'Farming before the Agricultural Revolution of the Eighteenth Century'.

7. The agrarian revolution in the eighteenth century—when and why. What it meant—new methods, enclosures.
8. New methods of cultivation. Jethro Tull—seed drill, horse-hoe, etc. Lord Townshend—four-year crop rotation, marling, drainage.
9. New methods of stock breeding. Bakewell, Coke, Colling Brothers.
10. Method of enclosing land. Advantages. Social hardship.
11. Some contemporary views on farming—Daniel Defoe, William Cobbett, Arthur Young.
12. Spread of information—Arthur Young. Board of Agriculture. Festivals.
13. Effect of war on English agriculture. The Corn Laws and eventual repeal.
14. The golden age of English agriculture (1850–75).
15. The Great Depression and measures to defeat it (1875–1900).
16. Agricultural workers' trade unions. The Tolpuddle Martyrs. Joseph Arch.
17. The First World War.
18. Inter-war measures. Subsidies. Boards, etc.
19. The Second World War.
20. Recent developments.

74   PROJECTS IN HISTORY

Recommended Books

Look at Farms, N. Dale (Hamish Hamilton)—rather simple
The Farmer, E. Holt (E.S.A.)—chapter on history of farming
Life and Work in England, Mrs H. A. L. Fisher (Edward Arnold)
A Short History of English Agriculture and Rural Life, C. J. Hall (Black)
Everyday Things in England series, C. H. B. and M. Quennell (Batsford)
The Medieval Village, M. E. Reeves (Longmans)
In Feudal Times, E. M. Tappan (Harrap)
Norman and Angevin, E. K. Milliken (Harrap)
Country Life Through the Ages, E. Boog-Watson and J. I. Carruthers (Allen & Unwin)
A Sense of History, Book 3, J. S. M. Smith (E. J. Arnold)
The Story of Agriculture, E. W. Burbridge (Pitman)
Pathways Through Time, Book I, T. G. Williams and E. W. Burbridge (Pitman)
An Introduction to Social History, C. R. Wright (Associated Newspapers Ltd)
We Were There, R. Power (Allen & Unwin)—Peasants' Revolt
We Too Were There, R. Power (Allen & Unwin)—Tolpuddle Martyrs
Rebels and Fugitives, F. Grice (Batsford)—on Peasants' Revolt and Tolpuddle Martyrs
Men Who Shaped the Future, E. Larsen (Phoenix House)—chapter on Harry Ferguson and agricultural tractors.
The Homeland Histories, Volume 5, W. J. Claxton (Wells Gardner, Darton)
Land, Trade and Travel, S. A. Williams (U.L.P.)
The Agrarian Revolution, J. Addy (Longmans)

Contemporary Accounts

Rural Rides, William Cobbett (Everyman)
Tour of Great Britain, Arthur Young
Horse Hoeing Husbandry, Jethro Tull

Brother to an Ox, F. Kitchen (Dent)—autobiography of a farm labourer
Life on the Land, F. Kitchen (Dent)

Fiction

Son of the Lane, I. Bolton (Blackwell)—Peasants' Revolt
Jockin the Jester, U. Moray-Williams (Chatto)—medieval peasant life
The novels of Adrian Bell—*Corduroy*, etc.
The novels of A. G. Street—*The Endless Furrow*; *Strawberry Roan*; etc. (Faber)

Sources of information

Ministry of Agriculture, Whitehall, London S.W.1
National Farmers' Union, Agriculture House, Knightsbridge, London S.W.1
National Union of Agricultural Workers, 308 Grays Inn Road, London W.C.1
National Federation of Young Farmers' Clubs, 55 Gower Street, London W.C.1

Museums

Science Museum, South Kensington, London S.W.7
Agricultural History Museum, Reading, Berkshire
The Curtis Museum, Shibden Hall, Halifax, Yorkshire
Cambridge Agricultural Institute, Cambridge
Agricultural Museum, Wye College, Wye, Kent
Rothamsted Experimental Agricultural Institute, Harpenden, Hertfordshire

The French Revolution

One of the epic periods in history which will appeal to children with a taste for the dramatic. The topic can be limited to the four years of the Revolution (1789–92) or it can be carried on to include Napoleon and the Revolutionary Wars and continue to 1815. The pupil should start by reading a brief account of the period in an encyclopaedia or in one or two textbooks on European history such as *Britain's Place in the World*, Book 3, by L. F. Hobley (Oliver & Boyd), *History of Britain and the World*, Book 4, by C. F. Strong (U.L.P.), or *A Practical Guide to Modern European History* by R. R. Sellman (Edward Arnold). A list of headings and a time-line and/or chronological list of the sequence of events might then be worked out, followed by a more detailed investigation of each section. Below is a scheme from which the teacher can suggest additions to the pupil's plan.

The teacher may also like to suggest that the pupil reads some of the many fictional accounts of this period. Even if they are historically inaccurate it will not matter as the pupil might include a brief 'review' of books read, pointing out the errors in emphasis or fact. A few historical novels are listed among the recommended books.

1. Picture of France before the Revolution. (a) France had been a leading military power for the last 150 years. Centralized despotic monarchy, with Ministers responsible to Crown alone, built up in the seventeenth century by Louis XIV and Cardinal Richelieu. During the eighteenth century Louis XV and Louis XVI weak, and their governments corrupt and inefficient. No representative national parliament. Taxation heaviest on peasants, inefficient and unfair—*gabelle* (salt tax), *taille* (property tax), *corvée* (forced labour), *octroi* (internal customs barriers). Peasants paid 80 per cent of their incomes in taxes, tithes and feudal dues. (b) Feudal system still in operation. Serfdom harshly maintained by absentee landlords. Aristocracy exempt from much taxation. (c) The Church exempt from taxation. Upper clergy rich and worldly. Heavy tithes exacted from the peasants.

2. Eighteenth-century growth of liberal ideas encouraged criticism of *Ancien Régime*. Influence of writers: (a) Voltaire. Attacks abuses, especially in the Church, in the satire *Candide*. (b) Montesquieu, *De L'Esprit des Lois*. Argued for limited monarchy

with separation of powers—legislature, executive and judiciary, each independent and acting as 'checks and balances' on each other. (Note this principle used in the United States Constitution.) (c) Rousseau's *Social Contract*. 'Man is born free but everywhere he is in chains.' Government should rest on the 'general will' of the people. (d) The Encyclopaedists: Diderot, etc. Writings criticized the French government.

3. Effect of the American Revolution. The successful revolt of citizens of British North America against an authoritarian government, and its new Constitution embodying the ideas of Rousseau and Montesquieu, encouraged French liberals to hope for similar developments in France.

4. Causes of French Revolution. (a) Abuses of the *Ancien Régime* as listed above and growth of liberal ideas and criticism. (b) Immediate causes. Financial and food crises. Indecision of Louis XVI in dealing with disorders or introducing moderate reforms.

5. Summoning of the States-General, 1789—had not met for 150 years. Nobles and clergy known as First and Second Estates; the Third Estate was the middle classes, workers and peasants. King agreed double representation for Third Estate. Disagreement about whether nobles, clergy and Third Estate should meet together. Third Estate claim to represent nation. Tennis Court Oath. Attempt to disband them. 'We are assembled by the national will and force alone shall disperse us' (Mirabeau). Clergy and some nobles join Third Estate.

6. Storming of the Bastille, 14 July 1789. Disorders in other areas. National Guard of citizens formed to govern Paris. On 4 August Louis XIV abolishes feudal privileges. Taxation reform. 'Liberty, equality, fraternity', the slogan of the Revolution.

7. Declaration of the Rights of Man.

8. Rule of National Assembly (1789–91), led by Mirabeau, aiming at constitutional monarchy on British pattern. Opposition from nobility who wanted to regain power and more extreme revolutionaries, Jacobins. 1791, death of Mirabeau. King and family try to escape from Paris, brought back by force.

9. 1792, invasion of France by Prussia and Austria to restore old order. Jacobin Revolution. King Louis suspended. Rule of Commune in Paris. Austrian and Prussian advance halted. Battle of Valmy. France declared a Republic. 1793, King and Queen guillotined.

10. Revolutionary leaders—Danton, Marat, St Just, Robespierre. 'Reign of Terror'. Hundreds of aristocrats and 'traitors' guillotined. Struggle for power between Danton and Robespierre. Overthrow of Robespierre and establishment of the more moderate 'Directorate'.

11. In 1799, ten years after the Revolution, Napoleon Bonaparte overthrows Directorate and re-establishes absolute power, but this time with support of middle classes and most of peasants.

12. Effects of French Revolution in France: (a) Equality before the law established. Privileges of clergy and nobles abolished. (b) Principle of absolute royal power overthrown (even if accepted for military expediency under Napoleon) and principle of popular sovereignty established. (c) End of feudalism. Break up of big estates into small peasant farms. (d) Unification of law and administration. *Code Napoléon*.

13. Effects of French Revolution on other countries—England, Austria, Germany, etc. Growth of nationalism, liberalism, political and social reform.

If the pupil has gone into this topic in any depth the study will probably end here with perhaps just a final paragraph or two about the Napoleonic Wars and what remained of the Revolution after 1815. If, on the other hand, the French Revolution has been given a less detailed treatment, then the pupil may like to continue his work with an account of the Revolutionary Wars:

14. 1792–5, defence of the Revolution from outside intervention and internal disaffection. In 1793, Britain, Prussia, Austria, Spain, Holland and Piedmont (First Coalition), all at war with France. Several anti-revolutionary risings in France. Invasion defeated by enthusiastic organization of New Republican Armies. Allies divided. First Coalition breaks up. Internal disaffection suppressed.

15. Second Coalition (Britain, Russia, Austria, Sicily, Portugal) broken up by Napoleon in 1801 after battle of Marengo. France supreme on land but Britain still dominant at sea. Peace Treaty of Amiens.
16. 1801, Bonaparte made Consul for life; 1804, made Emperor. Reorganization of France: improvements in transport, fairer taxation, foundation of Bank of France, national system of education, *Code Napoléon*.
17. 1803, Britain and France at war. Planned invasion of Britain. Third Coalition, 1805-7: Britain, Russia, Austria, Sweden and later Prussia. 1805, battle of Trafalgar—invasion plans defeated. Napoleon's victories at Austerlitz, Jena and Friedland. Britain almost alone.
18. Peninsular War, 1808-13.
19. Agreement between France and Russia, 1807, and breakdown, 1811. French attack on Russia, advance to Moscow. Disaster of retreat from Moscow, 1812.
20. Revolt of Prussians, defeated at Lutzen, but Prussians and Allies continue the fight. Invasion of France from Spain after success of Peninsular War. April 1813, Napoleon abdicates and is sent to island of Elba. Treaty of Paris, 1814, Louis XVIII restored.
21. The Hundred Days. Escape of Napoleon and return to France. Tries to make peace with Allies, but unwilling. Defeats Prussians at Ligny, but defeated by British and Prussians at Waterloo, 1815. Taken to St. Helena, dies 1821.
22. Settlement of 1815.

Recommended Books

The Book of Revolutions, B. Innes (Bancroft)
The French Revolution, 2 vols., R. Lacey (Jackdaw, Cape)
The French Revolution, A. Rosenthal (Longmans)
The Road to Modern Europe: 1789–1945, C. B. Firth (Ginn)
Europe: 1450–1815, E. J. Knapton (Murray)
A History of Modern Europe, 1789–1939, H. L. Peacock (Heinemann)

The True Book about the French Revolution, A. H. Booth (Muller)
A History of Modern France, Volumes 1 and 2, A. Cobban (Pelican)—
too difficult to read right through for all but very serious students,
but good for reference purposes and for chronological table of
events.
A History of Europe, Volume 2, H. A. L. Fisher (Eyre & Spottiswoode)
The French Revolution, D. I. Dowd (Cassell)

Fiction

Tale of Two Cities, Charles Dickens (Everyman and other editions)
The Scarlet Pimpernel, Baroness Orczy (Brockhampton)
Sir Isumbras at the Ford, D. K. Broster (Heinemann)
Chicot the Jester, Alexandre Dumas (Dent)
Scaramouche, Rafael Sabatini (Hutchinson)

Dictatorship

This is a topic in which a child might be encouraged to make a valuable comparative study of different types of dictatorship at different
times, after starting off perhaps with the more limited subject of the
rise of Hitler and/or Mussolini, a study of Russian Communism or
the lives of Cromwell, Nero or Charles I. From this wider look at an
abstract idea approached by comparisons of the history of various
dictators or dictatorships, an interesting and useful project could
be achieved.

One must first define the terms. What is meant by dictatorship,
and does it mean different things at different times? The child
should get a definition or definitions from a good dictionary and
from one or more of the children's encyclopaedias. A dictionary of
quotations may also provide some good ideas, for example: 'Dictators ride to and fro upon tigers which they dare not dismount. And
the tigers are getting hungry'—a very telling sub-heading for a

section on Mussolini, Julius Caesar or the South American dictators? These first definitions should lead to more words that may need defining—despotism, fascism, autocracy, etc.—and the teacher might suggest that a glossary of words should be compiled and set out in the project. A child capable of understanding some simple philosophical ideas might be encouraged to consult the index of a few books on political institutions such as R. H. S. Crossman's *Government and the Governed*, Shaw's *Everybody's Political What's What*, books by G. D. H. Cole, Professor Joad, etc., for useful ideas or quotations.

The next stage is to help in planning the shape of the project, which will clearly consist mainly of a series of studies of individual examples. The plan might be along these lines:

1. Definitions and glossary of terms.
2. List of examples that have been considered as dictatorships, whether or not the child considers the judgment justified— Alexander the Great, Julius Caesar, Nero, William the Conqueror, Cromwell, Charles I, Louis XIV, Peter the Great, Napoleon, Tsar Paul, the Kaiser, Hitler, Mussolini, Stalin, Tito, Nasser, Castro, etc.
3. Then the main part of the work should be a series of studies on as many as possible of the examples listed above. Some of these will have to be fairly brief as there is not much material, but others can be quite long accounts of the lives, ideas and methods of the dictators.
4. What, if any, qualities have these dictators or these systems in common and what are the differences? The child might consider one or two dictums in connection with each of the studies —Acton's 'Power corrupts and absolute power corrupts absolutely', and a dictator 'if weak is corrupted by his power, and if he is strong he is demented by it'. Get the child in this section to try and make a personal assessment of the various dictators and dictatorships he has considered.

The teacher may also like to suggest to the child that he explores the fact that dictatorships can be very dissimilar and that what constitutes a dictatorship can vary in different periods of history and as the climate of ideas changes. A dictator to some people is a strong and inspired leader to others, etc.

Recommended Books

Alexander the Great, E. H. Dance (Hutchinson)
Oliver Cromwell, S. Reed Brett (Black)
The True Book about Napoleon, A. Corley (Muller)
Napoleon, A. Cammiade (Methuen)
People and Power, K. Savage (Oxford)
The True Book about the Russian Revolution, J. Fisher (Muller)
Who's Who in History, ed. C. R. N. Routh (Blackwell)
Britain's Place in the World, Book 4, L. F. Hobley (Oliver & Boyd)
Three Dictators, S. King Hall (Faber)
Franco and the Spanish Civil War, L. E. Snellgrove (Longmans)
Modern Germany, R. Morgan (Hamish Hamilton)

Trade Unions and Working-class Movements

Very little has been written specially for children about trade unions, Chartism, the Co-operative movement, etc., and the child who chooses this subject will have to gather together his information from chapters in a number of social and economic textbooks. It is, however, a subject that can be done successfully, for instance, by a child who is developing an interest in political matters or one coming from a family active in trade union or political affairs.

The first step is to get the pupil to read an account of trade-union development from one or two simple textbooks such as *The Industrial Revolution* by M. E. Beggs Humphreys, *Our Democracy* by Rowland W. Purton, or *The New Outlook Histories*, Books 2 and 4. He should then set down in note form the basic facts or landmarks of the story and plan the main headings of his study. It would be quite reasonable, of course, to select a limited period or a special interest from the complete story. For instance, the study could be restricted to the history of unions for coal miners, dockers or transport workers; or a particularly dramatic phase could be studied in greater depth such as the Tolpuddle Martyrs, the Dockers' and Match Girls' Strikes, or the General Strike.

Once the main headings have been worked out the teacher can make suggestions about added sections or detail.

1. What trade unions are—a clear definition from a good dictionary and then a simpler description in own words. Comparison with medieval gilds.

2. When and why did trade unions start? This involves the child in writing a brief general account of the change from the domestic system to the factory system during the industrial revolution. (*Our People* by R. W. Purton (Collins), or other textbooks.)

3. The Combination Acts, 1799 and 1800. What they were and why they were passed. This involves a brief account of the fear and attitude of the Government and the upper classes towards the working classes as a result of the French Revolution. Therefore Trade Unions were illegal until—

4. Repeal of the Combination Acts, 1824. Work of Francis Place and Joseph Hume. After repeal, strikes and therefore the 1825 Act, 'no molestation or obstruction'.

5. Robert Owen and Grand National Consolidated Trade Union, 1834, and its collapse. At this point, if interested, the child could write not only about Owen and unions but also his many other causes—factory acts, co-operative societies, communities, education, etc.

6. The Tolpuddle Martyrs.

7. Chartism. After 1838 the Chartist movement absorbed the energy of many trade unionists. Brief account of the Charter and why it failed. (This could either be a few paragraphs or a longer study as set out below.)

8. The 'New Model' Trade Unions. The Amalgamated Society of Engineers, 1851. Description of type of members, type of work, aims, etc. How the trade unions became 'respectable'.

9. Trade unions made legal. The legislation of the 1870s.
10. Trade unions for unskilled workers: (a) Annie Besant and the Match Girls' Strike; (b) The Dockers' Strike.
11. Joseph Arch and unions for agricultural workers.
12. The Trades Union Congress and trade-union Members of Parliament.
13. Two set-backs and how they were overcome: (a) the Taff Vale Dispute; (b) the Osborne Judgement.
14. The General Strike. Full account of how it happened and the actual strike. Trades Dispute Act, 1927.
15. The Trade Union Act, 1945.
16. Trade unions today. Number of unions, membership, names of leaders, problem of unofficial strikes, etc. Recent proposals for trade-union legislation. Implications of wage freeze.

If trade unions are studied in detail there is enough material for a substantial project but some children may prefer to go into less detail and do instead some of the other aspects of working-class activity in the last 150 years. For example, Chartism might be given a longer treatment along these lines:

CHARTISM

1. The reasons for Chartism: disappointment about 1832 Reform Act; 1834 Poor Law Amendment Act; unions less popular after 1834 because of failure of G.N.C.T.U. and Tolpuddle Martyrs incident. General working-class discontent—housing, factory conditions, wages, cost of living.
2. The People's Charter—the six points.
3. The personalities: Francis Place, William Lovett, Fergus O'Connor.
4. Account of the progress of the movement. Presentation of first two petitions. Divisions between 'physical force' and 'constitutional means' point of view. Disputes within movement. Imprisonment of leaders.
5. Presentation of final petition. Fiasco of demonstration.
6. Reasons for collapse of Chartist movement. The Hungry Forties

and then improvements in standard of living. Chartism a 'bread-and-butter movement'.

Other subjects that could be included are the Co-operative Movement, Mechanics Institutes and Christian Socialism.

Recommended Books

The Chartists, P. Searby (Longmans)
Social and Industrial History of England, F. W. Tickner (Edward Arnold)
Our People and *Our Democracy*, R. W. Purton (Collins)
The Trade Unions, A. Robertson (Hamish Hamilton)
British Working Class Politics, G. D. H. Cole (Allen & Unwin)
Fifty Years March, F. Williams (Odhams)—especially Chapter IV
The General Strike, R. J. Cootes (Longmans)
The General Strike, J. Symons (Cresset)
Men who Fought for Freedom, E. Larsen (Phoenix House)—on the Tolpuddle Martyrs
A Century of Co-operation, G. D. H. Cole (Allen & Unwin)
We Too Were There, R. Power (Allen & Unwin)—on the Tolpuddle Martyrs
A Man's Life, J. Lawson (Hodder)—autobiography of trade unionist and labour leader
Strike or Bargain, D. J. Williams (Blond)
Protest, M. O'Connor (Blond)

Useful Addresses

Trades Union Congress, Great Russell Street, London W.C.1
Amalgamated Engineering Union, 110 Peckham Road, London S.E.15
National Union of Mineworkers, 222 Euston Road, London N.W.1
Transport and General Workers' Union, Transport House, Smith Square, London S.W.1
and the local offices of any of the big unions.
Fabian Society, 11 Dartmouth Street, London S.W.1—publishes tracts on Robert Owen, Francis Place, etc.

Museums

Co-operative Museum, Rochdale (where first Co-operative Society founded)

Robert Owen Memorial Museum, Newtown, Montgomeryshire

The Emancipation of Women

A possible subject for a keen feminist or perhaps for a suffragette's grandchild, who has been brought up with reminiscences of 'the cause' at home. Not much has been written for young people on this subject, so that anyone making this choice must be prepared to get the material from rather substantial works.

First, the pupil should read an account of women's suffrage in one or two of the good children's encyclopaedias and perhaps also the *Encyclopaedia Britannica* or Chambers' *Encyclopaedia*, and make notes about the main highlights and the chronology of the story. Then a skeleton plan should be prepared. A scheme from which the teacher can suggest additions to the pupil's plan is:

1. Early voices about the emancipation of women. Mary Godwin, Mary Wollstonecraft.

2. The struggle for votes for men. 1832 Reform Act only gave vote to five per cent of men. No question of women's vote. Chartism demanded manhood suffrage (though Lovett had originally suggested *universal* suffrage).

3. Legal and social position of women in the nineteenth century. Women in industry—factories and mines. Moves towards equality—women doctors, Florence Nightingale and nursing, etc.

4. Movement for women's suffrage dates from William Thompson's 'Appeal' for sexual equality, 1825. Cause taken up by Caroline Norton. John Stuart Mill and other radicals from the 1850s. Barbara Bodichon, Elizabeth Garrett Anderson, Emily Davies, Madame Belloc, Lydia Becker, etc. Presentation of Women's Suffrage Bills in Parliament. Public meetings, 1868

and 1869. Mr Richard Pankhurst. Mrs Fawcett. Support from Labour movement, Fabian Society, etc. Small advances in status of women in universities and professions. Votes for women ratepayers, 1869. Married Women's Property Act, 1882. In 1897 National Union of Women's Suffrage Societies, 500 affiliated societies—respectable, constitutional.

5. The Pankhurst family.

6. 1903, formation of Women's Social and Political Union. Meetings. Heckling and questions at meetings for General Election, 1906. Arrests for disturbances, prison rather than pay fines. Militancy begins. Processions, chaining to railings. Annie Kenney, Mrs Flora Drummond (the 'General'). Division of opinion between militant policy of W.S.P.U. and non-militant sides of movement. 1906, Mrs Pethick-Lawrence Treasurer of W.S.P.U., with steadying influence. Mrs Despard.

7. 1907, increase of public disorder. 'Mud March'. Campaign against Government. Liberal candidates at by-elections. Split in movement. Formation of Women's Freedom League (Mrs Despard)—less militant.

8. 1908–1909, disorders and skirmishes. Many prison sentences. First hunger striker (Miss Wallace-Dunlop), 1909. Forcible feeding. Lady Constance Lytton.

9. 1910, death of Edward VII. 1910, General Election. Mrs Pankhurst's group supported anti-Government candidates. Liberals lost 100 seats. Very narrow majority. Conciliation Committee of House of Commons (all parties) to further women's suffrage. Drafted Bill with votes for women with a property qualification—attacked by Lloyd George and Winston Churchill. Bill defeated. More disorders. Rough handling of women by police.

10. 1911, Conciliation Bill to give vote to some women promised but not fulfilled. Liberals intended to introduce universal suffrage but suffragettes wanted separate Bill for women's suffrage. Disorders again, stone-throwing and imprisonment. Some loss of public sympathy through militant tactics. Split between the Pankhursts (favoured extreme militancy) and the Pethick-Lawrences (more moderate). Party political divisions.

11. 1911, Franchise Bill introduced by Liberals to secure manhood suffrage (i.e. votes for servants, etc.), abolish plural voting, etc., and proposed to amend Bill to extend vote to women. But Speaker rejected an amendment that caused such a fundamental alteration to Bill. Private members' Bill on women's suffrage given time by Government, but defeated (by 48 votes), May 1913. New outbursts of militancy, including bombs, fires, etc. The 'Cat and Mouse' Bill. Emily Davison's suicide at the Derby under the King's horse, June 1913: great demonstration funeral procession. In 1914, continued, vigorous militancy, including attack on Buckingham Palace to petition the King. Disrespect for the courts.

12. August 1914, outbreak of First World War. Within a month militancy of suffragettes suspended, prisoners set free and suffragettes addressing recruiting meetings and in full support of war effort. In March 1917, Mr Asquith declared himself in favour of women's suffrage. Electoral Reform Bill passed in December 1917, and became law in January 1918. Gave vote to women over 30. November 1918, Bill passed enabling women to stand for House of Commons. Only one woman M.P. successful in December 1918 election—Countess Markievicz—a Sinn Feiner who never took her seat. Sixteen other women candidates.

13. 1928, age limit of 30 removed. 'Flappers' allowed to vote.

14. Effect of women having the vote. Influence 'conservative'. Number of women candidates, M.P.s, Cabinet Ministers. Why so few?

Recommended Books

Suffragettes and Votes for Women, L. E. Snellgrove (Longmans)
The Story of Mrs Pankhurst, J. Kamm (Methuen)
The True Book about Emmeline Pankhurst, H. Champion (Muller)
The Day Before Yesterday, ed. N. Streatfeild (Collins)
Rebels and Fugitives, F. Grice (Batsford)—chapter on 'Women in Revolt'
Votes for Women, R. Fulford (Faber)

Women in Revolt, J. Kazantzis (Jackdaw, Cape)
The Vote, J. Langdon-Davies (Jackdaw, Cape)
Unshackled, Dame Christabel Pankhurst (Hutchinson)
The Suffragette, Estelle Sylvia Pankhurst (Gay & Hancock)
Laugh a Defiance, M. R. Richardson (Weidenfeld)
The Cause, R. Strachey (Bell)
Elizabeth Garrett Anderson, J. Manton (Methuen)

Fiction

Fame is the Spur, Howard Spring (Collins)
Path-thro-the-Woods, Barbara Ker Wilson (Constable)

Poverty, Hardship and the Welfare State

This is a topic which might appeal to the idealistic child who is interested in social conditions and is moved by the story of misery in the past. It is one of those subjects that is not well covered by books specifically on this topic, but many general and economic history books must be consulted to piece together the story. It might be suggested first that the child should start by looking up: poverty; poor, the treatment of; the poor law, etc., in one of the children's encyclopaedias. He should then read the sections on the care of the poor in an elementary textbook such as *Our People* by R. W. Purton or the *New Outlook Histories*, Books 1 and 2, or in such books as *The Making of Modern Britain* by Derry and Jarman, *A Social and Economic History of Britain* by P. Gregg or *An Economic History of Britain* by Croome and Hammond. From these a skeleton plan of possible headings could be drawn up. From the following comprehensive scheme the teacher can advise the pupil about gaps in his outline or suggest new lines that might usefully be followed up:

1. Poverty in the Middle Ages. The Manorial System. The rôle of Church.

2. The break-up of the feudal system. Increased poverty in Tudor times. Dissolution of the monasteries. Enclosure of the land for sheep rearing. Increase in unemployment: rogues and vagabonds.

3. The Tudor Poor Law. Acts of 1531, 1572, 1597 and 1601. Houses of Correction. The rôle of Justices of the Peace. The parish made responsible for its own poor. Law of settlement and removal, 1662.

4. New problems of the eighteenth century. Upheavals due to agrarian and industrial revolutions. Workhouse Act, 1722.

5. A change in outlook. Gilbert's Act, 1782. The Speenhamland system, 1795, and its aftermath.

6. The Royal Commission on the Poor Law, 1832; the Poor Law Amendment Act, 1834. Edwin Chadwick. The public health movement.

7. Nineteenth-century treatment of the poor—Charles Dickens, Charles Reade, Charles Kingsley. Pauper apprentices—Health and Morals of Apprentices Act, 1802. Children in the care of Boards of Guardians.

8. The Royal Commission on the Poor Law, 1905; Majority and Minority Reports, 1909. Sidney and Beatrice Webb. Old Age Pensions Act, 1908. Lloyd George. National Health and Unemployment Insurance Acts, 1911. Labour Exchanges Act and Trade Boards Act, 1909.

9. Abolition of Boards of Guardians, 1929 and 1930. Public Assistance Committees, 1935. Unemployment Assistance Board.

10. Social security plans of Second World War. Beveridge Report, 1942. National Insurance Act, 1946. Family Allowances Act, 1945. National Insurance (Industrial Injuries) Act, 1946. National Health Service Act, 1946. National Assistance Act, 1948.

11. Recent developments in National Assistance. New ideas.

There are also other sub-headings that may be fitted in where the pupil wishes such as:

12. The care of old people.

13. Children in need of care. Orphans. Coram, Dr Barnardo.

Recommended Books

Poverty, G. Kent (Batsford)
The Industrial Revolution, 1760–1860, M. E. Beggs–Humphreys
    (Allen & Unwin)
Evidence in Pictures, I. Doncaster (Longmans)
The English Poor Law, J. J. and A. J. Bagley (Macmillan)
The Growth of the Welfare State, B. Druitt (Hamish Hamilton)
English Social History, G. M. Trevelyan (Longmans)
The Village Labourer, J. L. and B. Hammond (Longmans)
The Town Labourer, J. L. and B. Hammond (Longmans)
Select Economic Documents, Bland, Brown and Tawney (Bell)
London Labour and the London Poor, H. Mayhew (World's Classics)
Poverty, a Study of Town Life, B. S. Rowntree (Longmans)
Dr Barnardo, N. Wymer (Longmans)
Dr Barnardo, D. Ford (Black)
They Made History, Volume 3, H. Bellis (Cassell)—on Dr Barnardo
Six Reformers, J. Walton (Oxford)—Wilberforce, Peel, Fry, Shaftes-
    bury, Nightingale and Barnardo
The Story of Charles Dickens, E. Graham (Methuen)
The Coming of the Welfare State, Lady G. Williams (Allen & Unwin)
The Making of the Welfare State, R. J. Cootes (Longmans)
Human Documents of the Industrial Revolution and *Human Documents
    of the Victorian Golden Age*, E. R. Pyke (Allen & Unwin)

Fiction

Oliver Twist and other novels, Charles Dickens
Alton Locke, Charles Kingsley
Mary Barton, Mrs E. Gaskell—nineteenth-century poverty
The Coal Scuttle Bonnet, E. K. Seth Smith (Harrap)—a poor family
    in the nineteenth century

Sources of Information

Any local authorities for details of their current welfare services.
The L.C.C., for instance, published an illustrated booklet on their

Old People's Homes, which have now been taken over by the London Boroughs. Reports and publications of some of the voluntary societies concerned with this problem, e.g.:

Family Welfare Association, Denison House, Vauxhall Bridge Road, London S.W.1

National Council of Social Service, 26 Bedford Square, London W.C.1

Salvation Army, Men's Social Work, 110 Middlesex Street, London E.1

Salvation Army, Women's Social Work, 280 Mare Street, London E.8

Dr Barnardo's Homes, 18 Stepney Causeway, London E.1

Church of England Children's Society, Old Town Hall, Kennington, London S.E.11

Any pupil willing to go deeply into the subject might like to consult some of the classic official reports of the nineteenth and early twentieth centuries, e.g. *Royal Commission on the Poor Law, 1832–1834*; *Poor Law Commissioners on the Sanitary Condition of the Labouring Classes, 1843*; *Royal Commission on the Sanitary Condition of Large Towns and Populous Districts, 1842–1844*; *Royal Commission on the Poor Law and the Unemployed, 1905–1909*.

The Annual Reports of the Minister of Health, the Chief Medical Officer of the Ministry of Health, and the Chief Medical Officer of the Board of Education are also useful sources.

Life in Particular Periods

Possible subjects include life in Ancient Greece, Rome, Egypt; Anglo-Saxon England, the Vikings; the medieval village or town; the Crusades; life under the Tudors and/or Stuarts; Victorian England; the Inca Empire; the early history of America; the British in India, etc., etc. I have chosen as examples the medieval village and Victorian England.

THE MEDIEVAL VILLAGE

A straightforward subject but one which has the advantages of a complete entity and manageable proportions. One or two textbooks, such as *Our People* by R. W. Purton (Collins), or *The New Outlook History*, Book 1, by L. W. Cowie (Black), will serve as a guide for the main headings to be covered in the study. A good plan of a typical village is a first essential, and most of the recommended books at the end of this section include such a map. Suggested headings:

1. What the village looked like. England in Middle Ages much forested and with fairly isolated villages in clearings. Three big open fields divided into strips. Common. Church. Manor House. Villeins' plots. Map or diagram to illustrate this.

2. The Manorial System in England. Branch of feudalism—land held in return for service. Diagram to show pyramid nature of feudal system. King grants land to tenants-in-chief, who grant land to sub-tenants, who grant land to villeins in return for duties performed. Homage ceremony to overlord.

3. People of the Manor and their status in life. The Lord of the Manor and his family. The steward, bailiff, priest, reeve, the villeins and cottars, the serfs.

4. The rights and duties of villeins. *Rights*: to strips of land, common pasture, pannage (swine allowed to root in forest), turbary and estover (fuel for fire), public holidays. *Duties*: week work (usually to work three days a week on Lord's land), boon work (number of special days—harvest, etc.), cartage and cattle search, compulsory payments, gifts in kind, etc.

5. The manorial court officers: steward, bailiff, comptroller. Punishments: fossa and furca.

6. The three-field system of farming. Description of the normal farming year. One field ploughed in winter with wheat, one in spring with oats, beans, barley or rye, and one left fallow. Many animals killed off for winter. Implements used.

7. The manor house. Plan of typical manor house, description of furniture, etc.

8. The villeins' houses.
9. The church and the priest. Rôle of church in medieval village life. Payment of tithes to priest.
10. Clothes in the medieval village.
11. Food in the medieval village.
12. Sports and pastimes.
13. The Domesday survey. Entry in Domesday Book about a manor in the pupil's own district.

Recommended Books

The Medieval Village, M. E. Reeves (Longmans)
A Junior Sketch Map Economic History of Britain, I. Richards and J. A. Morris (Harrap)—very good map of village
The Middle Ages, R. J. Unstead (Black)—simple but good illustrations
Pathways Through Time, Book 2, E. W. Burbridge (Pitman)
Outlines of British Social History, E. H. Dance (Longmans)
Norman and Angevin, E. K. Milliken (Harrap)
The New Outlook History, Book 1, L. W. Cowie (Black)
Kings, Bishops, Knights and Pawns, R. Arnold (Constable)
A Portrait of the Middle Ages, M. R. Price (Oxford)
Redcap Runs Away, R. Power (Puffin)—fiction

Illustrative Material

Postcards of the Luttrell Psalter which provide an excellent picture of medieval farming can be obtained from the British Museum, London. Pupils might like to look at Domesday Book in the Public Records Office, Chancery Lane, London E.C.1, or to obtain from their local libraries a copy of the translated version of a manor nearest to their home.

VICTORIAN ENGLAND

This type of subject can be approached either by attempting to cover as many topics as possible within the period and thus presenting an overall picture, or by selecting 'Aspects of Victorian England', consisting of an entirely subjective choice of the kind of information that appeals to the individual researcher. I had a pupil recently, for example, who wrote an excellent and quite personal study of this period which she called 'We are not amused'. This dealt with a mixture of such horrific aspects of Victorian life as child labour, women in coal mines, noisome details of slum housing in the factory towns, public health and cholera, and also unusual comic items such as sea-bathing and bathing costumes, sport and women's clothes for sport—Mrs Bloomer—early cars and bicycles, some of the entertaining inventions shown at the Great Exhibition in 1851, and something about Queen Victoria's home life.

The first stage in this project should be to browse through one or two textbooks such as *The New Outlook History*, Book 4, by L. W. Cowie (Black), *A Portrait of Britain between the Exhibitions, 1851–1951*, by D. Lindsay and E. S. Washington (Oxford), A. B. Allen's *The Nineteenth Century up to 1850* and *Victorian England, 1850–1900* (Rockliff), or Rowland W. Purton's *Our Heritage* and *Our People* (Collins), and draw up a tentative list of topics to be covered. Then a start can be made on gathering material for any of the sections, not necessarily in any sort of chronological order. As the work progresses no doubt new lines of interest will develop and some of the original headings will be dropped. A time-line, either first or last in the study, is a useful device, and items can be added to it throughout. The time-line or chart could be set out under various headings, such as events in world history, inventions and discoveries, social reforms, political matters, etc.—or it could be a simple list of important events.

Amongst the headings could be:

1. Time diagram covering all aspects of Victorian era.
2. Britain in 1837. Results of Industrial Revolution to date.
3. Great discoveries and inventions. The age of steam. Improved transport—railways, steamships, internal combustion engine, bicycles, iron and steel, electricity. Effects on social life.
4. Queen Victoria: childhood, accession, views on political leaders and of duties of monarch, marriage and family, etc.

5. Town life. Descriptions of early housing and health conditions and improvements made. Chadwick, Octavia Hill.
6. Factory conditions. Legislation about children and women in factories and mines. Robert Owen, Lord Shaftesbury.
7. Treatment of the poor. Results of Poor Law Amendment Act. Dickensian workhouses.
8. Education. Development of a state system. Private schools.
9. Clothes.
10. Houses. Furniture. Domestic servants.
11. The right to vote. Reform Acts. Chartism. Trade Unions.
12. Writers of the Victorian period—Dickens, Thackeray, the Brontës, George Eliot.
13. Postal services, police, local government.
14. Medical advances—Simpson, Pasteur, Lister, Jenner, etc. Florence Nightingale and nursing.
15. The Great Exhibition, 1851.
16. The emancipation of women.
17. Brief biographies of some notable Victorian personalities, such as those mentioned above and Prince Albert, Peel, Palmerston, Disraeli, George Stephenson, Brunel, Faraday.
18. Leisure pursuits. Sport. Holidays, sea-bathing, etc.
19. Religion and doubt. The Evangelical Movement. The Oxford Movement. Cardinal Newman. Darwin's *Origin of Species*. Missionaries. Christian Socialists.
20. Foreign Affairs. Crimean War. The strengthening of the British Empire.

Recommended Books

Victoria's Reign, A. Cammiade (Methuen)
The New Outlook History, Book 4, L. W. Cowie (Black)
This England, Book 3, I. Tenen (Macmillan)
A Portrait of Britain from Peril to Pre-eminence, 1688–1851, D. Lindsay and E. S. Washington (Oxford)
A Portrait of Britain between the Exhibitions, 1851–1951, D. Lindsay and E. S. Washington (Oxford)

The 19th Century up to 1850, A. B. Allen (Rockliff)
Victorian England, 1850–1900, A. B. Allen (Rockliff)
The Industrial Revolution, 1760–1860, M. E. Beggs-Humphreys (Allen & Unwin)
English Life in the 19th Century, ed. G. A. Sambrook (Macmillan)
Select Economic Documents, Bland, Brown and Tawney (Bell)
The Last Hundred Years, C. H. C. Blount (Oxford)
Picture Source Book for Social History: Early 19th Century, M. Harrison and A. A. M. Wells (Allen & Unwin)
A History of Everyday Things in England, Volumes 3 and 4, M. and C. H. B. Quennell (Batsford)
London Life and the Great Exhibition, 1851, J. R. C. Yglesias (Longmans)
The Victorian Era, 1820–1901, E. K. Milliken (Harrap)
A Century of Change, 1837 to the Present Day, R. J. Unstead (Black)
Queen Victoria, A. H. Booth (Muller)

Fiction

The novels of Charles Dickens, esp. *Oliver Twist* and *Little Dorrit*
Mary Barton, Mrs E. Gaskell
Coningsby and *Sybil*, Benjamin Disraeli
Alton Locke and *The Water Babies*, Charles Kingsley
Shirley, Charlotte Brontë
Peril on the Iron Road, B. Carter (Hamish Hamilton)—building of the London–Birmingham Railway, 1836.
Hills of Sheep, E. Garnett (Hodder)—railway building in the Yorkshire Dales, 1869
Bridge under the Water, L. Meynell (Phoenix House)—Brunel and the Thames tunnel
Path-thro-the-Woods, B. K. Wilson (Constable)—woman nurse and doctor in the nineteenth century

Museums

London Museum, Kensington Palace, London w.8
Geffrye Museum, Kingsland Road, London E.2

The Rise of the U.S.A.

This is a topic which requires either a brief 'right-through' treatment or concentration on one or two sections, e.g. early settlement and colonization, the American War of Independence, the American Civil War, or the U.S.A. in the twentieth century. It is a subject that might well appeal to children who have enjoyed American films and are interested in finding out the real history behind the celluloid versions of 'how the West was won'. Children with relatives or pen friends in the U.S.A. might choose this subject and obtain good illustrative material from their contacts in the country. A useful selection might be made from the following comprehensive set of headings:

1. Map of the U.S.A. Main physical and climatic features, size. Present population.

2. Original inhabitants of U.S.A.: the Red Indians. Numbers when white men arrived and now. Various tribes and customs. Treatment of Red Indians by white men.

3. Early voyages to America—Vikings, Vinland Map.
Columbus and discovery of New World. Spanish Empire in Central and South America, Mexico and Florida. Cabot and Newfoundland. Drake and other sea-dogs attack Spanish treasure ships.

4. First English settlements. Virginia. The *Mayflower* and the Pilgrim Fathers. Reasons for early settlements—escape from religious persecution and escape from poverty in Old World. Therefore, strong spirit of liberty and independence. The establishment of the thirteen colonies: (a) northern colonies— New England colonies, including Massachusetts, Connecticut, etc. Puritan; (b) middle colonies—including Maryland (a Catholic settlement), Pennsylvania (Quaker, William Penn). Religious tolerance; (c) southern colonies—Georgia, North and South Carolina, etc. Mainly Anglican and Royalist. Plantations' need for slave labour.

5. The French explorers and settlements in Canada—Cartier, Champlain and La Salle. Competition between French Empire in interior and British colonies along coast. 1689–1748, three colonial wars between French and British (when French and British at war in Europe). French alliance with Indians. 1756–1763, French and Indian War (Seven Years War in Europe). Fort Duquesne. Montcalm. James Wolfe and fall of Quebec. Fall of Montreal. Treaty of Paris, 1763. French expelled from almost all Canada. France abandoned hope of colonial Empire in America.

6. The American Revolution. Britain tries to enforce Navigation Acts and Stamp Act, 1765, meets strong opposition. Cry of 'no taxation without representation'. The 'Boston Massacre', 1770. 'Boston Tea Party', 1773. The 'Intolerable Acts', 1774, passed by Britain.

7. War of Independence, 1775–1781. May 1775, George Washington commander of American army. Britain sends army to put down revolt. 4 July 1776, Declaration of Independence. Written by Thomas Jefferson—rights of men to 'life, liberty and the pursuit of happiness'. 1777, Americans defeat General Burgoyne at Saratoga. 1778, alliance with French and later Spanish and Dutch. 1781, Cornwallis surrenders at Yorktown. Independence of colonies recognized but British loyalists allowed to settle in Canada.

8. The creation of the Union. Weakness and problems of Congress government. 1787, Convention set up and agreed on the constitution of the United States of America. The Constitution. Independence of individual states, though certain powers (army and trade, etc.) given to the Federal Government. Federal Government by Congress of Senate and House of Representatives. Senate two members from each State, but membership of lower House by population. Office of President. Supreme Court.

9. Personalities of the New Republic. Brief biographies of George Washington, Thomas Jefferson, Alexander Hamilton. The Republican and Federalist Parties.

10. 1803, Louisiana Purchase from Napoleon Bonaparte (who got it from Spain) for 15 million dollars—doubled area of U.S.A.

11. The War of 1812. U.S.A. had stayed neutral during struggle between British and Napoleon and benefited from trade with both. But incidents between British Navy and American ships, also frontier war with Indians, believed to have been given British help. On land, American expedition against Canada very unsuccessful and in 1814 British raided Washington. On sea, Americans were successful. War ends when Napoleon defeated. 1819, Florida acquired from Spain. U.S. determination to have no interference from Europe with her affairs—Monroe Doctrine, 1823.

12. The moving frontier. Expansion westwards. 1789–1842, area of U.S.A. doubled, states increased from 13 to 26 and population from four to 16 millions. Constant arrival of immigrants from Europe. Gradual opening up, peopling and exploiting of lands to west of Alleghany Mountains—hardship, endurance, romance. Influence of the Frontier on American society.

13. Expansion of cotton growing in South after invention of Whitney's gin, 1793, and acquisition of Florida. Influence of the West on Government—Andrew Jackson, President 1829. Industrialization in America. Steam boats. Railways.

14. Slavery in the U.S.A. Negro slaves first brought over in early seventeenth century to work on cotton, sugar and tobacco plantations. Conditions under which they were brought. From 1781, with colonies gaining independence, each state could decide whether to have slavery within its borders or not. No great problem when only 13 states involved (five Southern states had slavery), but when Southern planters moved westward they wanted negro slaves to work for them there. Northern representatives disagreed. Wanted to have new States admitted to Union with slavery—Missouri and Texas.

15. U.S.A. acquires more territory, map to show this. Texas annexation. War with Mexico—Texas surrendered to U.S.A. in 1848, also all lands west of it including California. Oregon claimed by United States and Britain. 1846 treaty made boundary between

U.S.A. and Canada along the 49th parallel. 1848, gold rush to California.

16. 1850s, slavery issue important again. Moves towards Civil War. Abraham Lincoln and the Republican Party. John Brown's attack on arsenal at Harper's Ferry, Virginia. Brown hanged and becomes a martyr. Split in Democratic Party over protection of slavery throughout U.S.A. 1860, Lincoln elected President. 1861, seven slave-holding states—Texas, Louisiana, Mississippi, Alabama, Georgia, South Carolina and Florida—decide to leave the Union, declare themselves the Confederate States of America and Jefferson Davis their President. April 1861, Southern guns bombard Union's Fort Sumter.

17. The two sides in the Civil War. The North, 23 million people with big industrial resources but less good generals and much political intrigue. The South, nine million (3½ million of these negro slaves) poorly supplied but united, devoted to cause and well led.

18. The course of the Civil War, 1861–1865. In spite of inequalities between the two sides, war lasted four years. Three million men fought in it and 620,000 Americans died. Robert E. Lee. Ulysses S. Grant. General Sherman. Gettysburg. Assassination of Abraham Lincoln. Brief account of Lincoln's life.

19. Reconstruction of United States after war. Bitterness in Southern States. Ku Klux Klan. Prosperity in North.

20. Movement westward. Transcontinental railways—Union Pacific Company and Central Pacific Company. Map of chief railways by 1880s. Growth of population. Influx of European immigrants. Pioneers and the Wild West. The Mormons and Salt Lake City. Ranching, farming, mining. Subduing the Indians and giving them citizenship. End of the Frontier, 1890—whole American continent occupied.

21. American interests overseas. Purchase of Alaska from Russia. Interests in Pacific Ocean—Hawaii, Samoa. Spanish–American War, 1898. Fighting in China and Philippines. United States gained Philippines, Puerto Rico in West Indies and Guam in Pacific. Theodore Roosevelt's policy to make United States prosperous. The Panama Canal.

22. America and the First World War. Woodrow Wilson, President 1912–1920. United States neutral until 1917, when England and France at low ebb of fortune. Tide turned for Allies. November 1918, Armistice. President Wilson's Fourteen Points for Peace Settlement, chief point being the establishment of the League of Nations. But in United States opinion turned against Wilson; Senate rejected Treaty of Versailles and would not join League of Nations. Wilson defeated by Warren Harding for President.

23. Prohibition. 1920s great prosperity period of boom but ended in great depression of 1929. Widespread unemployment and misery. 1933, Franklin D. Roosevelt and New Deal. America between the Wars.

24. America and the Second World War. Isolationism. Lend-Lease Act. Atlantic Charter, 1941. December 1941, Japanese attack on Pearl Harbour. The United States take part in the Second World War.

25. U.S.A. 1945 to today. Harry Truman. War in Korea. President Eisenhower. U.S.A. and U.N.O. President Kennedy. Cuba. President Johnson. Vietnam. Black and White America.

Recommended Books

The Story of the American People, C. F. Strong (U.L.P.)
America—Yesterday and Today, C. F. Strong (U.L.P.)
The American Revolution, C. Clarke (Longmans)
The Epic of America, J. T. Adams (Routledge)
We the People, L. Huberman (Routledge)
A Brief History of the United States, A. Nevins (Oxford)
The American Civil War, A. H. Allt (Longmans)
The American Civil War, A. H. Booth (Muller)
The Oregon Trail, F. Parkman (Oxford)
The Mayflower and the Pilgrim Fathers; *The American Revolution*, J. Langdon-Davies (Jackdaws, Cape)
The U.S.A., A. Buchan (Oxford)
A History of the United States, C. P. Hill (Edward Arnold)
The U.S.A. Since the First World War, C. P. Hill (Allen & Unwin)

From Washington to Roosevelt, P. and L. Slosson (Ginn)
Makers of the U.S.A., J. Walton (Oxford)
The Growth of Modern America, A. E. Ecclestone (Bell)
Benjamin Franklin, R. McKnown (Black)
With La Salle Down the Mississippi, D. Sibley (Muller)

Fiction

Novels of Mary Johnston—*By Order of the Company*; *The Old Dominion*; *The Great Valley*; *Lewis Rand* and others
Pocahontas, David Garnett
Rabble in Arms and other novels, Kenneth Roberts
The Red Badge of Courage, Stephen Crane
Gone with the Wind, Margaret Mitchell
Uncle Tom's Cabin, Harriet Beecher Stowe
O, Pioneers, Willa Cather
Tom Sawyer and *Huckleberry Finn*, Mark Twain
Daniel Boone and other novels, S. E. White
Novels of Sinclair Lewis, such as *Babbitt* and *Main Street*
The Grapes of Wrath, etc., John Steinbeck
U.S.A., John Dos Passos
H. M. Pulham Esq., John P. Marquand
Wagons West, J. Craig
Indians, Indians, Indians, Phyllis R. Fenner
Child. n of the Oregon Trail, A. R. van der Loeff (Penguin)

Transport and Travel

A vast and well-documented subject from which the pupil must select the part which interests him most. He might begin by reading one or two of the general histories of transport such as *The Story of Transport* by C. Wise, *Transport, Trade and Travel through the Ages* by R. W. Morris or *Man Must Move*, by Laurie Lee and David Lambert, or looking up 'travel' and 'transport' in one or two encyclopaedias. Having got some idea of the different aspects of this subject the pupil can decide which items to include in his study, and over what period of time. Even if the pupil is going to concentrate on railways or motor cars it is a good idea to try and get him to see his topic in the context of man's increased mobility through the ages.

1. Man the wanderer. Man moves in search of food, trading, mating, fighting, visiting, adventure. Speed has increased from four miles an hour on foot to thousands of miles an hour in space. Ability to move loads has also increased from a few pounds carried on the back to the amount carried by a great freight train or ship.

2. Man moves via three main elements—A. Over land. B. On water. C. Through the air.

A. MOVEMENT OVER LAND: ROADS

(i) Early ways of carrying loads. First use of animals as beasts of burden. Early trackways.

(ii) Early vehicles. Sledges. The discovery of the wheel. Sumer. Chariots, wagons and carts.

(iii) Early road builders. Peru. China.

(iv) Roman roads: principles of road building. Diagram.

(v) Roads in the Dark Ages.

(vi) Roads in the Middle Ages. Medieval mud. Increase in trade and travel.

(vii) Roads in Tudor times. Pilgrims. Packhorses.

(viii) The Highway Act, 1555; parishes responsible for repair of roads. 1663, first Turnpike Act—tolls collected from road-users to pay for upkeep of roads.

(ix) General Wade's road building—result of 1715 Jacobite Rebellion.

(x) Turnpike Trusts in eighteenth century. Arthur Young's descriptions. Highwaymen.

(xi) John Metcalfe, 'Blind Jack of Knaresborough'. Plan of his roads with strong foundation, drainage, etc.

(xii) Carriages of eighteenth century—phaeton, gig, post-chaise, curricle, coach.

(xiii) First mail coach service, 1784. Palmer.

(xiv) John Macadam—early life. Repairing roads in Scotland. Surveyor in south of England. Macadam's principles of construction—diagram. Advantages of his system.

(xv) Thomas Telford—early life. Building roads, bridges and canals in Scotland. Menai Straits Suspension Bridge. Telford's principles of construction—diagram.

(xvi) The golden age of coaching, 1820–35. Stage and mail coaches. Coaching inns, etc. Speeding up of travel—quote figures.

(xvii) The coming of the railway. By 1850 coaching days over and railway in place. In 1860s steam carriages on roads but Parliament imposed speed and safety limits—man in front with red flag and therefore steam carriages disappeared. Roads little used and Turnpike Trusts disappeared.

(xviii) The coming of the bicycle. The 'hobby-horse', 'penny-farthing' and the 'safety bicycle'. (Clothes for bicycling—Mrs Bloomer.)

(xix) The coming of the motor car. Siegfried Marcus, Carl Benz, Gottlieb Daimler—1880s in Germany. In France, Panhard and Levassor. In U.S.A., Henry Ford. Development slow in England because of 'Red Flag' Act. Early cars—Sunbeam, Napier, Swift, Argyll and Singer. Petrol-driven, steam and electric cars.

(xx) Roads in the twentieth century, the Ministry of Transport. Serious problems of traffic congestion. The new motorways. The Buchanan Report.

Recommended Books

Man Must Move, L. Lee and D. Lambert (Rathbone)
The Story of Britain's Highways, R. Syme (Pitman)
Wheels on the Road, S. E. Ellacott (Methuen)—excellent general account
The Story of the Highway, A. Allen (Faber)

The Story of the Road, J. W. Gregory (Black)
Transport, R. A. S. Hennessey (Batsford)
Transport, Trade and Travel through the Ages, R. W. Morris (Allen & Unwin)
Transport by Land, T. Insull (Murray)
The Discovery Book of Motors, J. Anderson (Harrap)—very simple
The Story of Transport, C. Wise (Oxford)
Men Who Changed the World, E. Larsen (Phoenix)—chapters on John Boyd Dunlop, Henry Ford
Seven Civil Engineers, J. Walton (Oxford)—chapter on Macadam
Travel and Transport Through the Ages, N. E. Lee (Cambridge)— very good general introduction
Transport, E. Larsen (Phoenix)—modern developments
Discovering Roads and Bridges, M. O. Greenwood (U.L.P.)
Roads and Streets, P. Thornhill (Methuen)
From Steamcarts to Minicars, L. E. Snellgrove (Longmans)
The Story of the Motor Car, J. A. Roy (Pergamon)
The Motor Revolution, D. H. Thomas (Longmans)
The Study Book of Roads, G. Middleton (Bodley Head)
Motor Cars, L. T. C. Rolt (E.S.A.)
The Boy's Book of Motors, K. B. Hopfinger (Burke)
Bridges and Roads, E. de Maré (Faber)
Bridges, L. Fry (Methuen)

A. MOVEMENT OVER LAND: RAILWAYS

(i) Early wooden rail or track ways, used in mines for coal or metal-ore wagons. Trucks pushed or pulled by men, later pulled by horses. Iron covering on rails. First cast-iron rails, Coalbrookdale, 1777. Use of flanged wheels—diagram. 1801, Surrey Iron Railway—first public railway along which people could pay to haul their goods.

(ii) Steam locomotives and carriages. After James Watt patented his steam engine, 1769, steam power used for variety of purposes. Nicholas Cugnot's steam carriage frightened people of Paris. William Murdoch's steam locomotive, followed up by Richard Trevithick's locomotive in use in South Wales, also

'Catch as Catch Can' in Euston Road. Locomotives built by Trevithick in use at Wylam Colliery, near Newcastle. Blenkinsop's Rack Locomotive. Hedley's 'Puffing Billy', 1813, and 'Wylam Dilly'.

(iii) George Stephenson.

(a) Brief account of his life. Worked as engineman at colliery near Wylam, studied Wylam locomotives. Urged his colliery owners to use locomotive he designed. Produced 'Blucher', 1814—drew load of 30 tons at five m.p.h. Soon improved on this. Engineered a two-mile line from colliery to River Wear.

(b) Stockton–Darlington line. Stephenson invited to engineer this line by Edward Pease. Intended only for goods but Stephenson urged that it should also be allowed to carry passengers. Stephenson built locomotives and engineered the line. First public passenger railway opened, September 1825. 'Locomotion', speed 12 m.p.h. (c) Liverpool–Manchester line. Stephenson asked to engineer this. Difficult crossing of bog (Chat Moss), also mile-long tunnel and long viaduct. The Rainhill Trials—prize of £500 for best locomotive. Four entries, but Stephenson's 'Rocket' at 30 m.p.h. easily the best. Opening of Liverpool–Manchester line—death of Huskisson.

(iv) Widespread development of railways. Problems over Acts of Parliament, obstruction of landowners, etc. But within ten years of Liverpool–Manchester railway most of larger towns in England linked by railway.

(v) 'Railway mania'. George Hudson the 'Railway King'.

(vi) Early railway carriages. Signalling systems.

(vii) The battle of the gauges. Stephenson v. Brunel.

(viii) I. K. Brunel—brief account of life and engineering achievements.

(ix) Social benefits of railways.

(x) Railway companies amalgamated, 1923—London Midland and Scottish, London and North Eastern Railway, Southern, and Great Western.

(xi) Some great locomotives—'Silver Link', 'Coronation Scot', etc. Records.

(xii) Railways today. Railways nationalized January 1948, now British Rail. Disappearance of steam locomotive. Diesels. Electrification.

Recommended Books

Railways for Britain, P. Thornhill (Methuen)
Railways of Britain, C. J. Allen (Nelson)
The Story of British Locomotives, R. B. Way (Methuen)
Look at Railways, L. T. C. Rolt (Hamish Hamilton)
Railways, L. Fry (E.S.A.)
The British Railway Locomotive, 1803–1853, G. F. Westcott (H.M.S.O.)
—excellent illustrations
Discovering Railways, G. R. Halson (U.L.P.)

B. MOVEMENT ON WATER: INLAND WATERWAYS

1. River navigation in early times. Rafts, canoes and coracles. Viking raiders sailed up English rivers in long-boats. Sailing barges, wherries.
2. Importance of navigable rivers in England in Middle Ages. Improvements in river navigation—dredging, weirs, etc.
3. Coming of canals in Britain. Well-known earlier on Continent. First important English canal built for Duke of Bridgwater by James Brindley from Duke's coal mine in Worsley to Manchester—Barton aqueduct, an engineering feat. Cut price of coal in Manchester by half. Later extended to mouth of Mersey. Brindley built more canals: Grand Trunk linking Trent and Mersey, important for Pottery industry; Staffordshire and Worcestershire canal, etc. Soon canal system crossed England linking Hull, London, Liverpool and Bristol by water. Leeds–Liverpool canal. Grand Junction canal. Kennet and Avon. Shropshire Union. Ellesmere canal, etc.
4. Canal mania. 1790–1794, hundreds of canal schemes. Many never built but some did very well.

5. Other canal builders: Robert Whitworth (pupil of Brindley), William Jessop, John Rennie, Thomas Telford, John Smeaton.
6. Coming of the railways and decline of canals.

Recommended Books

Look at Canals, L. T. C. Rolt (Hamish Hamilton)
The Study Book of Canals, G. Middleton (Bodley Head)
Inland Waterways, L. T. C. Rolt (E.S.A.)

B. MOVEMENT ON WATER: TRAVEL BY SEA

1. The first ships. Dug-out canoes, guffas, coracles, Egyptian reed boats.
2. Early Egyptian sailing and rowing boats, 4000–1500 B.C. Phoenician sailors and ships, seventh century B.C.
3. Greek ships—galleys with sails. Warships and merchant ships (fourth to fifth centuries B.C.).
4. Rome and Carthage.
5. Norse long-ships.
6. King Alfred's navy.
7. The Norman fleet—detail of ships from Bayeux Tapestry.
8. Developments in ship construction: the castled ship, rudders, bowsprits, lateen sails, carracks, caravels.
9. The great voyages of discovery of the fifteenth century—improvements in ships and navigational instruments.
10. Sixteenth-century struggle for supremacy at sea between Spain and England. Galleons. Voyages of Sir Francis Drake and Magellan. The Spanish Armada.
11. Ships of the seventeenth century. East Indiamen. The *Mayflower*. Trade with the New World expands.
12. Eighteenth-century warships. The struggle between England and France. The great days of Nelson.
13. Food at sea. Scurvy and the end of this disease.
14. Nineteenth century. The clippers. The tea races. The Atlantic packets. The last days of sail.

15. The coming of steam ships. Early paddle steamers. William Symington's *Charlotte Dundas*, Robert Fulton's *Clermont*, Henry Bell's *Comet*.
16. The first ocean-going steamships. 1819, *Savannah* crossed Atlantic using steam and sails. 1831, *Royal William* crossed Atlantic using only steam.
17. Brunel's *Great Western*. The shipping lines—Cunard, P. & O., etc.
18. The screw. Brunel's *Great Britain*—first screw-driven ship to cross Atlantic. Iron ships instead of wooden hulls. Brunel's *Great Eastern*.
19. The steam turbine (Charles Parsons).
20. Steam ships change to oil from coal. Diesel engines. Turbo-electric ships.
21. Submarines.
22. Naval developments in the nineteenth and twentieth centuries. The ironclads. The *Dreadnought*. The First World War.
23. Twentieth-century liners. The Blue Riband.

Recommended Books

The Story of Ships, S. E. Ellacott (Methuen)
Ships and Seamen, D. Clark (Longmans)
Discovering Sailing Ships, C. R. France (U.L.P.)
Sailing Ships: their history and development as illustrated by the collection of ship-models in the Science Museum (H.M.S.O.)
Transport by Sea, T. Insull (Murray)
Ships, A. B. Cornwell (E.S.A.)
Travel by Sea through the Ages, R. J. Hoare (Black)
The Real Book of Ships, I. Block (Dobson)

Great Lives

'History is the essence of innumerable biographies', said Thomas Carlyle, so it is perhaps not surprising that many children when

asked to select a subject for a history project choose the life of one
or more of the great names of the past—Alfred the Great, Queen
Elizabeth I, Joan of Arc, Nelson, Florence Nightingale, the Duke of
Wellington, etc. They usually choose a well-known character whom
they admire for bravery or humanity, though their choice may also
be influenced by the feeling that this will be a straightforward assignment. Left to themselves they will get 'a book' on this hero or
heroine and will settle down to reducing it into a careful chronological account of the events in this 'great life'. Teachers may find it
hard to be enthusiastic when the well-worn names crop up again but
they should try not to be too discouraging. After all, to quote
Carlyle again, 'A well written life is almost as good as a well spent
one'. Teachers should rather try to show the pupil ways of extending
a simple biography to make the study more interesting.

Instead, for example, of Napoleon alone, a more lively project
might compare the careers and achievements of Napoleon and Wellington, or Napoleon and Hitler. Great commanders in different
periods—Alexander the Great, Julius Caesar, the Duke of Marlborough, Napoleon, Wellington, Foch or General Eisenhower—
might be contrasted along with some kind of consideration of the
changes in the problems that they faced.

A number of different kinds of people who were contemporaries
might be grouped together—great names of Tudor times (Queen
Elizabeth I, Shakespeare, Raleigh, Bacon, Mary Queen of Scots,
etc.) or eminent Victorians (Stephenson, Queen Victoria, Owen,
Dickens, Disraeli, Darwin, Annie Besant, etc.). A geographical
link—great names of Yorkshire or Wales or Birmingham—might
provide an interesting piece of research and could be set in a background of local history.

Another way to group biographies is by the achievements they
represent in a particular field; great inventors, doctors, explorers,
and so on. The project seems to me to have more merit if it is not a
random selection of names but has a linking thread, such as great
statesmen or teachers or scientists, so that some sort of comparative
assessment of their contribution can be made. As well as the obvious
link of the same profession or being alive at the same time, the

people chosen could have some common quality—bravery, humanity, rebelliousness, curiosity or the spirit of adventure—and the subjective individual choice of names is then an interesting aspect of the work. The personal choice of the authors of two recent books —*Heroes and History* by Rosemary Sutcliff and *Rebels and Fugitives* by F. Grice—for example, involves not only a number of interesting lives but also a consideration of the qualities of heroism and the reasons for revolt. Occasionally a pupil chooses a rag-bag of personal heroes and heroines for which the only theme could be 'people I admire', but here a good introduction giving reasons for the selection and a conclusion contrasting their qualities and successes could give the work some coherence and point.

Sometimes the life to be studied is connected with a particular subject, and the project can be extended to cover the character's interest more fully. For example, 'Florence Nightingale and Nursing' could deal with her life and a study of nursing services right up to the present day, or an account of Lord Shaftesbury could not only . deal with all the reforming causes of his career but could follow up more recent developments in child welfare or factory legislation.

Another way of making a study of an individual less limited is to write about the 'Life and Times' of the person concerned. Thus a selection of relevant social history—clothes, houses, furniture, food, etc., or major historical events—could be sketched in as a background to the life of a famous person. 'The Life and Times of Joan of Arc', for instance, could include an exposition on the reasons for the Hundred Years War, a section on the feudal system in France, the church, castles, armour and weapons, etc., and even houses, clothes and food. Good studies of the 'Life and Times . . .' kind can be done about such characters as Chaucer, Shakespeare, Dr Johnson, Samuel Pepys and William Cobbett, where personality and period can make a harmonious piece of work.

Museums

There are a number of museums devoted to famous people, and many local museums have some mementoes of well-known local

personages. Among the museums in which information on famous
people in history can be found are:
Admiral Blake and the Duke of Monmouth Museum, Bridgwater,
  Somerset
Andrew Carnegie Birthplace Memorial, Dunfermline
Joseph Chamberlain Memorial Museum, Birmingham
Richard Cobden: Dunford House, Heyshott, Nr. Midhurst, Sussex
James Cook: Museum of Literary and Philosophical Society, Whit-
  by, Yorkshire
Samuel Crompton: Hall i' th' Wood Museum, Bolton
Oliver Cromwell: Cromwell Museum, Market Square, Huntingdon
Grace Darling Museum, Bamburgh, Northumberland
Charles Darwin: Downe House, Downe, Kent
Charles Dickens: Dickens House, 48 Doughty Street, London
  W.C.1
  Dickens Birthplace Museum, 393 Commercial Road, Portsmouth
Benjamin Disraeli: Hughenden Manor, High Wycombe, Bucking-
  hamshire
Francis Drake: Buckland Abbey and Tythe Barn, Plymouth
David Livingstone: Scottish National Memorial, Blantyre
Thomas More: Tudor Barn Art Gallery, Well Hall, Eltham,
  Middlesex
Horatio Nelson: Victory Museum, Portsmouth
  Nelson Museum, Glendower Street, Monmouth
Isaac Newton: The Museum, Grantham
Florence Nightingale: Claydon House, Claydon, Nr. Winslow,
  Buckinghamshire
Robert Owen Memorial Museum, Newtown, Montgomeryshire
Cecil Rhodes Memorial Museum, Bishop's Stortford
Robert Scott: Polar Research Institute, Cambridge
George Washington: Sulgrave Manor, Nr. Banbury, Oxfordshire
James Watt: Watt Institute, 15 Kelly Street, Greenock
Duke of Wellington: Apsley House, Hyde Park Corner, London
John Wesley: 47 City Road, London E.C.1
William Wilberforce: Wilberforce House, Hull
General Wolfe: Quebec House, Westerham, Kent

There are also museums connected with various well-known writers and artists of the past which may be of interest for period studies:

Jane Austen's House, Chawton, Hampshire

The Brontë Parsonage Museum, Haworth, near Keighley, Yorkshire

John Bunyan: Bedford Public Library

Lord Byron: Newstead Abbey, Nottinghamshire

Thomas Carlyle: Cheyne Row, Chelsea, and Ecclefechan, Scotland

S. T. Coleridge's Cottage, Nether Stowey, Somerset

Edward Elgar's House, Broadheath, near Worcester

Thomas Hardy: Dorset County Museum, Dorchester

Dr Johnson's House, Lichfield, and Gough Square, London

John Keats's House, Keats Grove, London N.W.3

John Milton's Cottage, Chalfont St Giles, Buckinghamshire

William Morris Gallery, Walthamstow, London E.17

John Ruskin Gallery, Bembridge, Isle of Wight, and Museum, Brantwood, Coniston, Lancashire

Walter Scott Museum, Canongate, Edinburgh 8

William Shakespeare: Birthplace and New Place, Stratford-on-Avon; Anne Hathaway's Cottage, Shottery, Warwickshire; Mary Arden's House, Wilmcote, Warwickshire

Robert Louis Stevenson Memorial House, Howard Place, Edinburgh

Izaak Walton Museum, Shallowford, Staffordshire

William Wordsworth Museum, and Dove Cottage, Grasmere

Books

No list of books is given here as the number is so vast, and children can easily find what they need in the biographical section of the library.

Books on Museums and Other Places to Visit

There are several publications that it is most helpful to have on the shelves of the school library or the history library for consultation about good places to visit for history project work. Often useful places quite near at hand are not known about by children, and family expeditions or holiday visits can be planned if details of the place and its subject matter are available. The most obvious books are the guides to buildings and sites maintained by the Ministry of Works which can be obtained from H.M. Stationery Office, London, or from local curators, and many other provincial museums or buildings publish guide-books which can be obtained locally.

Books on Museums include:

Going to Museums, J. Palmer (Phoenix House)
Museums, ed. Sir Hugh Casson (National Benzole Books)
Museums and Galleries in Great Britain and Ireland (Index Publishers Ltd)
The Libraries, Museums and Art Galleries Year Book
Museums and Young People (UNESCO)

General Books of Reference

The *Encyclopaedia Britannica*, *Chambers' Encyclopaedia*, the *Dictionary of National Biography*, etc., are useful for consultation on particular points but are not presented in a very palatable form for children. There are, however, several children's encyclopaedias that are invaluable, especially for the early planning stages of a project. The best of them are:

Oxford Junior Encyclopaedia (Oxford)
Children's Britannica (Encyclopaedia Britannica Ltd)
Book of Knowledge (Waverley Book Co.)
Knowledge (Purnell)—issued as a weekly magazine but also sold in bound volumes
Everyman's Encyclopaedia (Dent)—an adult encyclopaedia that children can use readily.

Other good books or series of books helpful on many topics include:

Muir's Historical Atlas, Medieval and Modern, ed. G. Goodhall and R. F. Treharne (George Philip)
Chambers' Biographical Dictionary, ed. W. Geddie and J. Liddell (Chambers)
A History of the English People, J. J. Mitchell and M. D. R. Leys (Longmans)—English life from the Stone Age to First World War
Reign by Reign, S. Usherwood (Michael Joseph)
Illustrated English Social History, G. M. Trevelyan (Longmans or Pelican)
A History of Everyday Things in England, Volumes I–IV, C. H. B. and M. Quennell (Batsford)—also other volumes by these authors

A Social and Economic History of Britain, P. Gregg (Harrap)

The Picture Source Books for Social History series (Allen & Unwin)

The Rockliff New Project series

This England, Books 1–3, I. Tenen (Macmillan)—useful for drawings of tools, machinery, etc.

A Portrait of Britain in the Middle Ages, M. R. Price (Oxford)

A Portrait of Britain under the Tudors and Stuarts, M. R. Price and C. Mather (Oxford)

A Portrait of Britain from Peril to Pre-eminence, 1688–1850, D. Lindsay and E. S. Washington (Oxford)

A Portrait of Britain between the Exhibitions 1851–1951, D. Lindsay and E. S. Washington (Oxford)

A General History of England 1832–1960, Barker, St Aubyn and Ollard (Black)

A Sketch Map Economic History of Britain, J. L. Gayler and I. Richards (Harrap)

Living and Working. A Social and Economic History of England, 1760–1960, L. F. Hobley (Oxford)

The Twentieth Century, R. S. Lambert (Grant)

Modern Times, I. M. M. MacPhail (Arnold)

An Illustrated History of Modern Europe 1789–1945, D. Richards (Longmans)

An Introduction to Social History, C. R. Wright (Associated Newspapers)

An Illustrated History of Science, F. Sherwood Taylor (Heinemann)

They Saw It Happen series (Blackwell)

Evidence in Pictures series, I. Doncaster (Longmans)

The History Bookshelf series (Ginn)

This Is Your Century, G. Trease (Heinemann)

How They Lived series (Blackwell)

Between the Wars, P. Hastings (Benn)

History for Today series, T. H. McGuffie (Macmillan)

Historical Fiction

A GOOD WAY to get the 'feel' of a period being studied for a project is by reading some of the excellent historical fiction written for children. The pupil must recognize, of course, that these books *are* fiction, but that many of them are very accurate in the historical background detail that they provide. Books of this kind should be included in the bibliography of the project and short reviews or criticisms of relevant novels might well be included in the study.

Ancient Times to Norman Conquest

Abrahall, C. H., *Boadicea, Queen of the Iceni* (Harrap)

Baker, George, *Golden Dragon* (Lutterworth)—Alfred the Great
  Hawk of Normandy (Lutterworth)—William the Conqueror

Boucher, Alan, *The Path of the Raven*; *The Wineland Venture*; and *The Greenland Farers* (Constable)—Vikings

Bryher, *The Roman Wall* (Collins)—adventures of Roman boys among Picts north of Hadrian's Wall
  Fourteenth of October (Collins)—battle of Hastings

Clark, Pauline, *Torolv the Fearless* (Faber)—Vikings

Durant, G. M., *Fires of Revolt* (Bell)—Boadicea's times

Gray, Ernest A., *Roman Eagle, Celtic Hawk* (Bodley Head)—1st century A.D.

Green, Roger Lancelyn, *The Land Beyond the North* (Bodley Head)—the Argonauts

Heyer, Georgette, *The Conqueror* (Heinemann)—William I

Hodges, C. Walter, *The Namesake* (Bell)—King Alfred

Kipling, Rudyard, *Puck of Pook's Hill* (Macmillan)

Lytton, Lord, *The Last Days of Pompeii* (Collins)

Meynell, Lawrence, *Under the Hollies* (Oxford)—Roman occupation of Britain and other periods

Mitchison, Naomi, *The Conquered* (Cape)—Caesar's Conquest of Gaul
The Land the Ravens Found (Collins)—Norse settlement in Britain
Muntz, Hope, *The Golden Warrior* (Chatto)—Harold Godwinson
Oliver, Jane, *The Eaglet and the Angry Dove* (Macmillan)—Scotland in the Dark Ages
Oman, Carola, *Alfred, King of the English* (Dent)
Pardoe, M., *Argle's Oracle* (Routledge)—Celtic Britain
Parker, Richard, *The Sword of Ganelon* (Collins)—9th-century Danish invasions
Perkins, Lucy, *The Cave Twins* (Cape)
Reason, Joyce, *Swords of Iron* (Phoenix House)—Iron-Age Britain
Bran the Bronze-smith (Dent)—lake village near Glastonbury before the Romans
Schmeltzer, Kurt, *The Axe of Bronze* (Constable)—Stonehenge
Seaby, Allan, *The Ninth Legion* (Harrap)—Roman Britain
Alfred's Jewel (Harrap)
Seton, Anya, *The Mistletoe and the Sword* (Brockhampton)—Boadicea
Severn, Dorothy, *Kerin the Watcher* (Dent)—250-B.C. Britain
Speare, Elizabeth George, *The Bronze Bow* (Gollancz)—Roman Britain
Sutcliff, R., *The Eagle of the Ninth* (Oxford)—Roman Britain
The Outcast (Oxford)—Romans
The Silver Branch (Oxford)—Romans
The Shield Ring (Oxford)—Vikings
Dawn Wind (Oxford)—6th-century Britain
The Lantern Bearers (Oxford)—Roman Britain
Warrior Scarlet (Oxford)—Bronze Age
Trease, Geoffrey, *Crown of Violet* (Macmillan)—Ancient Greece
Word to Caesar (Macmillan)—Roman Britain
Mist over Athelney (Macmillan)—Alfred the Great
The Secret Fiord (Macmillan)—Vikings
Treece, Henry, *Legions of the Eagle* (Bodley Head)—Caractacus
The Eagles have Flown (Bodley Head)—6th century A.D.
War Dog (Bodley Head)—Roman Britain

Great Captains (Bodley Head)—King Arthur's knights
Hounds of the King (Bodley Head)—battle of Hastings
Men of the Hills (Bodley Head)—Ancient Britain
Viking's Dawn (Bodley Head)
The Road to Miklagard (Bodley Head)—Vikings
The Splintered Sword (Bodley Head)—Vikings
Golden Strangers (Bodley Head)—coming of Bronze Age people to
Britain
Trevor, Meriol, *The New People* (Macmillan)—coming of the Anglo-
Saxons
Wallace, Lew, *Ben Hur* (Collins)—1st-century-A.D. Palestine

The Middle Ages

Adams, Doris Sutcliffe, *Desert Leopard* (Hodder & Stoughton)—
Crusades
de Angeli, Marguerite, *The Door in the Wall* (World's Work)
Baker, George, *Leopard's Cub* (Lutterworth)—Black Prince
Barringer, Leslie, *The Rose in Splendour* (Phoenix House)—Wars of
the Roses
Baumann, Hans, *The Barque of Brothers* (Oxford)—voyages of dis-
covery of 15th century
Bolton, Ivy, *Son of the Land* (Blackwell)—serf in Peasants'
Revolt
Chute, Marchette, *The Innocent Way-faring* (Phoenix House)—
Chaucer's England
Clark, Pauline, *The Boy with the Erpingham Hood* (Faber)—young
archer at Agincourt
Doyle, Sir Arthur Conan, *Sir Nigel* (Murray)
The White Company (Murray)
Elliott, L. S., *Fear in the Forest* (Warne)—time of William I
In Freedom's Cause (Warne)—Simon de Montfort
The Miller and his Family (Warne)—Edward III's time
Fairless, M., *The Gathering of Brother Hilarius* (Duckworth)—Black
Death

Garrad, Phillis, *The Book of Ralf* (Bell)—life of a Norman boy

Garrett, Henry, *Thirteen Banners* (Bodley Head)—Simon de Montfort's rebellion of 1265

Gilbert, Jane, *Imps and Angels* (Warne)—building of Lincoln Cathedral in the 13th century

Gray, Elizabeth J., *Adam of the Road* (Black)—13th century

Harnett, Cynthia, *The Woolpack* (Methuen)—15th-century wool trade

   Ring Out Bow Bells (Methuen)—London of Henry V

   The Load of Unicorn (Methuen)—Caxton

Hyam, Freda, *Who's For the North* (Phoenix House)—battle of Otterburn

Jowett, Eleanore, *Told on the King's Highway* (Harrap)

King-Hall, M., *Jehan the Ready Fist* (Puffin)—Crusades

Lewis, Hilda, *The Gentle Falcon* (Oxford)—Richard II himself

Lindsay, Jack, *Nine Days a Hero* (Dennis Dobson)—Wat Tyler

Maugham, A. Margery, *Monmouth Harry* (Hodder & Stoughton) Henry V and Agincourt

Meyler, Eileen, *Castle on the Rock* (Epworth)—Corfe Castle prior to the Hundred Years War

Meynell, Lawrence, *Young Master Carver* (Phoenix House)— Edward III's reign

Moray-Williams, U., *Jockin the Jester* (Chatto)—14th-century peasants and nobles

   The Noble Hawks (Hamish Hamilton)—14th-century Welsh Marches

Oliver, Jane, *Young Man with a Sword* (Macmillan)—Robert Bruce

   Faraway Princess (Macmillan)—11th-century England and Scotland

Oman, Carola, *Crouchback* (Hodder & Stoughton)—Richard III

   Ferry the Fearless (Pitman)—life in a medieval castle, Richard I

   Jonel (Pitman)—sequel, younger children

Picard, Barbara L., *Ransom for a Knight* (Oxford)—children travel to Scotland to ransom their father captured at Bannockburn

Porter, Jane, *Scottish Chiefs* (Puffin)—Wallace, and fight against Edward I

Power, Rhoda, *Redcap Runs Away* (Puffin)—medieval town and village life
  We Were There (Allen & Unwin)
Price, Christine, *Three Golden Nobles* (Bodley Head)—children
Reason, Joyce, *The Secret Fortress* (Dent)—William Rufus
  The Mad Miller of Wareham (Dent)—King John
Rush, Philip, *The Minstrel Knight* (Collins)
  A Cage of Falcons (Collins)—15th-century London
  King of the Castle (Collins)—Wat Tyler's rebellion
  Queen's Treason (Collins)—Queen Isabella's revolt against Edward II
Scott Daniell, David, *The Boy They Made King* (Oxford)—Lambert Simnel
Scott, Sir Walter, *Ivanhoe* (Collins)—knights and tournaments, Richard I
Seth Smith, E. K., *The Black Tower* (Harrap)—Wars of the Roses
  At the Sign of the Gilded Shoe (Harrap)—the Black Prince
Stevenson, R. L., *The Black Arrow* (Collins)—Wars of the Roses
Strong, L. A. G., *King Richard's Land* (Dent)—Peasants' Revolt
Stuart, D. M., *The Young Clavengers* (U.L.P.)—14th century
Sturt, M., and Oakden, E. C., *Tales of the Canterbury Pilgrims* (Dent)
Sutcliff, R., *The Chronicle of Robin Hood* (Oxford)
  Knight's Fee (Oxford)
Tey, Josephine, *Daughter of Time* (Penguin)—Richard III
Trease, G., *The Baron's Hostage* (Phoenix House)—13th-century England, Simon de Montfort
Trevor, Meriol, *Merlin's Ring* (Collins)
Welch, R., *The Gauntlet* (Oxford)—Welsh border country in feudal England
  Knight Crusader (Oxford)—Crusades

Tudors and Stuarts

Ashton, Agnes, *Water for London* (Epworth)—piping water into London in 17th century
Bell, Douglas, *Drake was my Captain* (Warne)—Elizabethan seamen

Blackmore, R. D., *Lorna Doone* (Dent)—West Country in time of Charles II and James II

Boxer, Cecile F., *Little Girl with a Bell* (Muller)—Restoration London

Charlton, Moyra, *Wind from Spain* (Macmillan)—Scotland in 17th century

Child, William, *In the Wake of Rebellion* (Warne)—civil law, Judge Jeffreys

Chute, Marchette, *The Wonderful Winter* (Phoenix House)—boy actor in Shakespeare's London

Dallow, M., *Heir of Charlcote* (Puffin)—Tudor theatre

Dawlish, P., *He Went with Drake* (Harrap)

Dymoke, Juliet, *The Orange Sash* (Jarrolds)—families divided in the Civil War

Edmonston, C. M., and Hyde, H. L. F., *His Majesty's Players* (Harrap)—17th-century theatre and Court

Elliott, L. S., *The Mercer Family* (Warne)—Restoration period

Evans, J. R., *The Boyhood of Shakespeare* (Hutchinson)

Fidler, Kathleen, *I Rode with the Covenanters* (Lutterworth)—Scottish Presbyterians in reign of Charles II

Forester, C. S., *Earthly Paradise* (Michael Joseph)—Columbus

Gaggin, E. R., *Down Ryton Water* (Harrap)—Pilgrim Fathers

Garrett, Henry, *Gamble for a Throne* (Bodley Head)—Civil War

Harnett, Cynthia, *The Great House* (Methuen)—1690s
Stars of Fortune (Methuen)—plot to free Princess Elizabeth from Woodstock

Hodges, C. W., *Columbus Sails* (Bell)

Irwin, Margaret, *The Stranger Prince; Royal Flush;* and *The Proud Servant* (Chatto)—Civil War and Restoration

Kent, L. A., *He Went with Magellan* and *He Went with Vasco da Gama* (Harrap)

King-Hall, Magdalen, *Sturdy Rogue* (Nelson)—Elizabethan England and the Armada

Kingsley, Charles, *Westward Ho!* (Everyman)—Armada

Lane, Jane, *The Escape of the King* (Evans)—Charles II after Worcester

Lewis, C. Day, *Dick Willoughby* (Blackwell)—Spanish main, Mary Stuart, etc.

Leyland, Eric, *Fire Over London* (Hutchinson)—1666

Marryat, Captain, *Children of the New Forest* (Collins)—Civil War, Royalist children in hiding

Masefield, John, *Martin Hyde* (Longmans)—Duke of Monmouth

Niven, John, *The Young Inverey* (Faber)—Jacobites

Nolan, Winefride, *David and Jonathan* (Macmillan)—Roman Catholic family after Gunpowder Plot

Exiles Come Home (Macmillan)—Roman Catholic family in reign of James I

Rich Inheritance (Macmillan)—Catholic recusancy in reign of Elizabeth

Oliver, Jane, *Mine is the Kingdom* (Collins)—James I

Bonfire in the Wind (Macmillan)—Scotland in 17th century, Covenanters

Parker, Richard, *The Three Pebbles* (Collins)—adventure in the time of John Hawkins

Quiller-Couch, Sir A., *The Splendid Spur* (Dent)—Royalist view of Civil War

Reed, M. Baines, *The Gate House* (Edward Arnold)—Elizabeth I

Rice, Dorothy, *Hugh Nameless* (Blackie)—Fire of London

Ross, Sutherland, *A Vagabond Treasure* (Hodder & Stoughton)—Civil War

A Masque of Traitors (Hodder & Stoughton)—Babington Plot, 1582

The Sword is King (Hodder & Stoughton)—Civil War

Scott, Sir W., *The Fortunes of Nigel* (Macmillan)—London of James I

Scott Daniell, D., *Hunt Royal* (Puffin)—Civil War

Speare, Elizabeth George, *The Witch of Blackbird Pond* (Gollancz)—17th-century England

Strong, L. A. G., *The Fifth of November* (Dent)

Sutcliff, R., *The Queen Elizabeth Story* (Oxford)

Brother Dusty Feet (Oxford)—Tudor Theatre

The Armourer's House (Oxford)—Henry VIII

Simon (Oxford)—Civil War, division within families, etc.

Trease, G., *Trumpets in the West* (Blackwell)—Civil War and Restoration

Cue for Treason (Blackwell)—travelling actors in Elizabethan England

The Silver Guard (Blackwell)—events leading to Civil War, Puritan sympathies

The Grey Adventurer (Blackwell)—Fire of London and settlement in Carolinas

Treece, H., *Wickham of the Armada* (Hulton)—boy actor in Elizabethan London and the Armada

Twain, Mark, *The Prince and the Pauper* (Chatto)—a London waif and Edward VI

Upson, Dorothy B., *Elizabethan Adventure* (Hutchinson)—plot on life of Elizabeth I

Utley, Alison, *A Traveller in Time* (Faber)—Mary Queen of Scots

Vipont, Charles, *The Heir of Craigs* (Oxford)—Jacobite intrigue

Welch, Ronald, *For the King* (Oxford)—Civil War

Wibberley, Leonard, *The King's Beard* (Faber)—Elizabethan sea adventures, attack on Cadiz

Wood, Andrew S., *Beat the Drum* (Hodder & Stoughton)—Elizabethan seadogs

Wood, W. H., *The House in the Sea* (Harrap)—building the Eddystone lighthouse, late 17th century

Eighteenth and Nineteenth Centuries

Armstrong, Thomas, *The Crowthers of Bankdam* (Collins)—Yorkshire woollen manufacturer's family, 19th–20th century

King Cotton (Collins)—Lancashire during the American Civil War

Bennett, Arnold, *The Card*; *Clayhanger* (Methuen)—life in the 19th century

Bentley, Phyllis, *The Adventures of Tom Leigh* (Macdonald)—woollen cloth trade in early 18th-century Yorkshire

Broster, D. K., *The Flight of the Heron* (Heinemann)—Jacobites

The Gleam in the North (Heinemann)—Jacobites

The Dark Mile (Heinemann)—Jacobites

Sir Isumbras at the Ford (Heinemann)—French Revolution

Ships in the Bay (Heinemann)—Wales in French Revolutionary Wars

Buchan, John, *Midwinter* (Nelson)—Jacobite rising, 1745

Burton, Hester, *Time of Trial* (Oxford)—early 19th-century social conditions

Castors Away (Oxford)—time of the battle of Trafalgar

Carter, Bruce, *Peril on the Iron Road* (Hamish Hamilton)—railways in 19th century

Castle, Douglas, *Sword of Adventure* (Blackie)—Yorkshire boy's adventures in London in 1720s

Chadwick, Doris, *John of the Sirius* (Nelson)—early settlers in Australia

Cheeseman, Evelyn, *Landfall the Unknown* (Puffin)—Australia in 18th century

Coatsworth, Elizabeth, *The Last Fort* (Hamish Hamilton)—French Canada after fall of Quebec

Cooper, James Fenimore, *The Last of the Mohicans* (Collins)—French and English wars in 18th-century America, life of Red Indians and frontiersmen

Craig, J., *Wagons West* (Dent)—trek from Missouri to Oregon during opening up of the American Mid-West

Dumas, Alexandre, *Chicot the Jester* (Dent)—French Revolution

Fidler, Kathleen, *The Droving Lad* (Lutterworth)—cattle driving in Scotland in early 19th century

Fitzroy, Olivia, *The Hunted Head* (Cape)—Bonnie Prince Charlie

Forbes, Esther, *Johnny Tremaine* (Constable)—American War of Independence

Forester, C. S., *Mr. Midshipman Hornblower* and all the Hornblower novels (Michael Joseph)—Napoleonic Wars

Death to the French (Bodley Head)—very accurate picture of naval and military life in 19th century

The Gun (Bodley Head)—Peninsular War

Garnett, Emmeline, *Hills of Sheep* (Hodder & Stoughton)—railways in the 1870s

Garrett, Henry, *Rough Brown Waters* (Bodley Head)—19th-century piracy and smuggling
Secret of the Rocks (Bodley Head)—19th-century railway building in Yorkshire

Gunn, James, *Sea Menace* (Constable)—19th-century voyage to Australia

Hackforth-Jones, Gilbert, *Hurricane Harbour* (Hodder & Stoughton) —Nelson at Antigua

Hayes, John F., *Buckskin Colonist* (Blackwell)—early 19th-century settlers in Canada

Howard, Elizabeth, *Beside Lake Michigan* (Bodley Head)— Amerca, mid-19th century

Jackson, H., *The Sign of the Glove* (Blackie)—Cornwall in George III's reign

Kamm, J., *He Sailed with Captain Cook* (Harrap)

Knight, Frank, *The Golden Monkey* (Macmillan)—sailing clipper to Australia in 1850s
Clippers to China (Macmillan)—tea-clippers of 1860s
The Bluenose Pirate (Macmillan)—American emigrants of 1830s
The Partick Steamboat (Macmillan)—early Clyde steamships

Lane, Jane, *The Escape of the Prince* (Evans)—Bonnie Prince Charlie

Marryat, Captain, *Mr Midshipman Easy* and *Masterman Ready* (Collins)—19th-century sea experiences

Meynell, Lawrence, *Bridge Under the Water* (Phoenix House)—the younger Brunel and Thames tunnel

Quiller-Couch, Sir A., *Fort Amity* (Dent)—French Canadian life in time of Wolfe and Montcalm

Robertson, Wilfred, *The Blue Waggon* (Oxford)—Great Boer Trek, 1836, Capetown to Natal

Rochester, G., *Drums of War* (Warne)—American Civil War

Ross, Sutherland, *Freedom is the Prize* (Hodder & Stoughton)— American War of Independence
Three Steps to Tyburn (Hodder & Stoughton)—18th-century London

Sabatini, R., *Scaramouche* (Hutchinson)—French Revolution

Selby-Lowndes, Joan, *Night Hawk* (Collins)—innkeeper's family in late 18th-century London

Seth Smith, E. K., *The Coal Scuttle Bonnet* (Harrap)—a poor family in 19th century

Smith, C. Fox, *Knave-Go-By* (Oxford)—West of England, mid-19th century

The Valiant Sailor (Oxford)—sailor in Napoleonic War

Stevenson, R. L., *St Ives* (Everyman)—England and Scotland in the Napoleonic Wars

Stuart, D. M., *The Children's Chronicle* (U.L.P.)

Syme, Ronald, *Gipsy Michael* (Hodder & Stoughton)—19th-century New Zealand

The Forest Fighters (Hodder & Stoughton)—American War of Independence

Island of Revolt (Hodder & Stoughton)—Revolt of negro slaves, 1796, in Grenada

Thackeray, W. M., *Vanity Fair* (Macdonald)—English at time of Battle of Waterloo

Welch, Ronald, *Escape from France* (Oxford)—French Revolution

Captain of Foot (Oxford)—Napoleonic Wars

Captain of Dragoons (Oxford)—Duke of Marlborough's campaigns

Mohawk Valley (Oxford)—English campaign against the French in Canada in 18th century

Wibberley, Leonard, *The Wound of Peter Wayne* (Faber)—American Civil War

Wilson, Barbara Ker, *Path-thro'-the-Woods* (Constable)—Victorian girl struggles to become a doctor